How to teach and assess

HISTORY

in the National Curriculum

TEACHING HISTORY
RESEARCH GROUP

Heinemann Educational,
a division of Heinemann Educational Books Ltd,
Halley Court, Jordan Hill, Oxford OX2 8EJ

OXFORD   LONDON   EDINBURGH
MADRID   ATHENS   BOLOGNA   PARIS
MELBOURNE   SYDNEY   AUCKLAND   SINGAPORE
TOKYO   IBADAN   NAIROBI   HARARE
GABORONE   PORTSMOUTH NH (USA)

First published 1991

**British Library Cataloguing in Publication Data is
available on request from the British Library**

ISBN 0 435 31072 0

Designed by Gecko Limited, Bicester, Oxon
Printed in Great Britain
by Thomson Litho Ltd, East Kilbride, Scotland

ACKNOWLEDGEMENTS
We are grateful to the headteachers, staff and pupils of the
following schools for permission to include material:

Beck Row Primary School, Suffolk
Belthorn County Primary School, Blackburn, Lancs
Ercall Wood School, Telford
Lakenheath Primary School, Suffolk
Laughton Endowed Primary School, Lincs
Ludlow School, Shropshire
Marsden County Primary School, Nelson, Lancs
Monks Abbey School, Lincoln
The National School, Grantham, Lincs
Primet County High School, Colne, Lancs
St Mary's C.E. Primary School, Mildenhall, Suffolk
St Michael's School, Burton Park, West Sussex
Southlands High School, Chorley, Lancs
Waterloo County Primary School, Blackpool, Lancs

We also wish to thank Dr Geoff Timmins of Lancashire
Polytechnic for the material on 'The Turnpike Road'.

Thanks are also due to the following for permission to include
material:
Bradford Central Library for Figure 34
Hodder & Stoughton Publishers for Figure 24
Lancashire County Library for Figure 25
Lancashire County Record Office for Figures 22,23
Ordnance Survey for the map on which Figure 33 is based
Phillimore & Co. Ltd for Figure 28.

CONTENTS

The Teaching History Reseach Group

Martin Booth (Chairman), Lecturer in Education, University of Cambridge
Christopher Culpin, GCSE Chief Examiner and author
Rachel Hamer, Head of History, St Michael's School, Burton Park, West Sussex
Terry Lewis, Headteacher, Mildenhall Upper School, Suffolk
Tim Lomas, Education Inspector (History), Lincolnshire
Henry Macintosh, Consultant, Assessment and Accreditation, Education Division, Department of Employment
Rosemary Rees, Assistant Secretary YHREB (NEA) and author
Joe Scott (Secretary), author
Margo Scott, Deputy Headteacher, Sandhurst County Primary School, Kent
Paul Shuter, History Publisher, Heinemann Educational
Sue Styles, County Adviser (History), Lancashire. GCSE Chief Examiner and author

INTRODUCTION

This book sets out to advise teachers on the first three key stages of National Curriculum history, on which they are already embarked. Now that the Statutory Order has emerged from the avalanche of paper about history teaching, teachers urgently need to adapt work they are already doing and to design new work to fit the new framework. We offer detailed suggestions on planning, teaching and assessment, based in the main on plans made in a variety of schools up and down the country, and on discussions with teachers and advisers. We are grateful for this help, and list in the acknowledgements the schools which have kindly allowed us to use their work.

The first chapter of the book deals with strategic planning of a whole year's or term's work. The second discusses the difficulty of making sure that assessment identifies and encourages pupil progress, and suggests one way in which this may be done. The third chapter, 'Teaching and Assessing', makes suggestions about the planning, teaching and assessment of individual topics. The final chapter discusses some of the many ways in which local history can be used in all key stages.

We have not dealt with each key stage in its own separate chapter. A welcome feature of the history National Curriculum is that it looks at school history as a whole, and sets out a framework to help teachers at each stage to build on the work their pupils have already done. To do this they need to know what that work is. They need to know, too, what historical knowledge and understanding their pupils will want in order to build in later key stages on the foundations already laid. The reader is recommended to look through the whole book, and not just at those parts labelled with a specific key stage. In this way the book can help to provide common ground between colleagues who in turn teach the same pupils at different stages, and to encourage and inform discussion between them.

1 PLANNING THE KEY STAGES

Teachers need to draw up a plan for each key stage so that they can be sure to provide the right balance and coherence between the different types of history within it, and the right progression over the two, three or four years which the key stage will cover. They should be clear how history in Key Stage 1 will be integrated over reception, Y1 and Y2 with other National Curriculum subjects. They should decide the timing of the core units, especially in Key Stage 2, and the selection of supplementary units, especially in Key Stage 3. They may wish to combine some units with other units. There is plenty of room for manoeuvre, but this makes planning essential, so that teachers can provide, and be seen to provide, the whole National Curriculum, but within its framework can find elbow-room for their own professional creativity.

Planning Key Stage 1

The Statutory Order (page 13) specifies that, 'Pupils should be given opportunities to develop an awareness of the past and of the ways in which it was different from the present'; and it lays down five key elements:

1 The use of historical stories from different cultures and periods.

2 The use of different types of historical sources.

3 The investigation of people's way of life in recent and more remote times – to include their everyday life, work, leisure and culture.

4 The teaching of the lives of famous men and women – such as rulers, saints, explorers and inventors.

5 The study of historical events, ceremonies and anniversaries which have been remembered for generations, such as the Olympic Games and the Gunpowder Plot.

To make sure that these requirements are met, all teachers involved in Key Stage 1 need to make time to plan together what they intend to teach. They each need to know what the others are covering or intend to cover so that pupils don't miss some areas or cover others twice. At the end of a term teachers should meet again to discuss what they actually did and how it worked. In this way they become aware of what each class is covering and they can exchange ideas and resources so that everyone benefits. If working in a primary school, then Key Stage 2 teachers should also be involved, so that they are aware of what has been covered lower down the school.

Some questions to consider

1 Is there enough 'historical' material in our schemes of work? If there is not enough in one topic area, can we compensate by putting more in another?

2 Are there enough different types of historical resources available for the pupils to use? Key Stage 1 as a whole should include :

- artefacts;

- pictures and photographs;

- music;

- adults talking about their own past;

- written sources;

- buildings and sites;

- computer-based material.

3 Have we covered a wide range of different periods, cultures, famous people and past events? Have we covered everyday life in the past, 'ordinary' people as well as famous and royal ones? Have we included people who can talk to pupils about the past, such as grandparents or the education officers of local museums?

4 Does our planning allow for progression? How do we slot into our teaching plan pupils moving from another school?

5 Are we meeting the three attainment targets? If not, where do we need to improve?

6 How do we assess what we have taught? How do we assess in a way which is not too time-consuming? How do we assess fairly for all pupils?

7 How do we introduce history to pupils in the reception class in a way that they can understand?

A suggested check-list

When planning history teaching for Key Stage 1, teachers need to refer to the five 'key elements' (Order, page 13) to make sure they are all included. By checking weekly they can quickly see what they have and have not covered, and by checking termly or even half-termly they can see what attainment targets have and have not been met. This is bound to take time at first. The check-list in Figure 1 may help teachers to make their initial plan and also to see at a glance what has been done and what remains to be covered.

Year group	What has been covered?	Date
Topic/subject area:		
Awareness of different periods and cultures using stories:		
Myths and legends		
Historical events		
Eyewitness accounts		
Fictional stories		
Range of historical sources:		
Artefacts		
Pictures and photographs		
Music		
Adults talking about their own past		
Written sources		
Buildings and sites		
Computer-based material		
Everyday life, work, culture and leisure:		
Local changes in children's and other people's lives		
Changes in lives of people since the Second World War		
Lives of people beyond living memory		
Famous men and women		
Past events:		
Local and national		
Other countries		
Remembered by succeeding generations		
Comments		
Links with other subject areas:		
Maths		
Science		
English		
Geography		
Music		
Others		

Figure 1 *Suggested check-list for teaching history at Key Stage 1.*

Planning Key Stage 2

Topic work and the study units

History in years 3–6 has hitherto largely been organised within thematic topics. Many schools are already planning termly or half-termly themes which embrace all the statutory curriculum areas, each of which has a particular subject emphasis. How should we select material to use for such topics/themes?

Core units   The core units do not leave much room for manoeuvre, especially for teachers who want to take a largely chronological approach. Suggestions are given in Chapter 3, pp. 43 and 44 for 'history-led' topics and 'history-emerging' topics. It will be essential to flag the topics in some such way, and also to flag the history elements within them if teachers are to be sure that they have covered the content requirements of the National Curriculum.

Supplementary units   There should be no problem in adapting those supplementary study units which fit in with existing themes. It is essential, however, not to dismantle study units, so that pupils can grasp essential long-term ideas like development.

Units which won't fit into topics   Some pieces may not fit, however hard teachers try. Some schools are deciding that a limited number of aspects of history will look so artificial in any recognised topic that they must be treated separately. Others intend to separate the core units and place those supplementary units which fit into whole or part curriculum topics.

Choosing supplementary study units

Choose units which fit in with existing thematic topics. For instance, 'Ships and Seafarers' or 'Houses and Places of Worship' will fit easily into technology-led topics. The local history unit is another that can be tailored to fit in easily with other subject areas.

Don't worry if some units cover only some of the 'perspectives' (political, economic, technological, etc.) set out on page 15 of the Order. The requirement is for 'substantial attention to each perspective across the key stage' (page 16). As long as an overall balance across the four years of Key Stage 2 is provided, individual units may emphasise those elements which help them to link to other work.

Mixed-age classes

Teachers may find it possible to teach different history to pupils of different ages who are within the same key stage. Those with a class that cuts across the key stages will have to do this. Most teachers, however, will be able to choose units which can be taught to pupils of different ages working together, but with tasks planned appropriate to each pupil. National Curriculum history has the advantage of attainment targets without content in them. This means that teachers of mixed-age classes can cover the same content with all members of the class, but then set work around the particular statements of attainment which are most appropriate for the age and progress of different individuals or groups. It should be easy enough to tailor the teaching units to the needs of a mixed-age class. The Order does not insist that particular units must be covered at particular ages or in a given order. Whatever the approach adopted it will be important to make sure that each individual pupil follows a coherent and progressive course.

Other planning points Make sure that the work will bring pupils into contact with a *range of historical sources* (documents, printed sources, artefacts, pictures, music, buildings, oral sources). Selection of source material may be made with an eye to links with other parts of the overall syllabus, e.g. statistical source material linking to mathematical awareness or written sources to work in English.

Avoid the 'lucky dip' approach – picking out historical material that happens to fit in with something else, but without considering the need for coherence of the history as a whole. Pupils need:

- to be introduced fairly regularly to work that they identify as 'history';

- to have the best idea they can of what history is – that it is about people and about events in the past, that it is based on evidence, and that it is a tentative account to be considered rather than a true story to be learned;

- to build up in their minds some coherent map of the past.

Aim clearly to develop a progressive historical understanding over the four years. Planning and delivery should aim to:

- develop an understanding of the ideas of cause, motive and consequence;

- help pupils to recognise and understand different viewpoints and different interpretations of events;

- help them to use, interpret and evaluate sources;

- improve their ability to select the more from the less important;

- help them to imagine historical situations and to see that history is different from fiction because of the way history must be based on evidence.

- develop their ability to make connections, comparisons and relationships between the different facets of history;

- help them to plan and to communicate meaning in history, e.g. by asking simple questions, posing and testing simple hypotheses, pursuing their own simple historical investigations.

Don't assume that pupils know nothing already – they get most of their historical awareness and knowledge from their lives outside the classroom.

Don't underestimate what pupils can do. It isn't true that pupils under 11 can't think, explain, understand time and change, or use and evaluate evidence. Six-year-olds can already grasp relationships and make comparisons. With clear targeting of skills and concepts, Key Stage 2 can lead them a long way.

Planning Key Stage 3

The course should be a balanced one (see 'key elements', Order, pages 33 – 4). The scheme of work over the whole key stage should make sure that pupils study 'from a variety of perspectives'.

Some basic principles

There is no need to include all of the perspectives mentioned in every study unit – it is the broad balance that is essential. The appropriate 'perspective' should be written into the scheme of work where it best exemplifies the developments of the period studied.

Give pupils 'opportunities to explore links between history and other subjects, develop information technology capability, and develop knowledge, understanding and skills related to cross-curricular themes,' (see 'General Requirements', Order, page 11). Write explicit reference to links of this sort into schemes of work. See pages 13 and 14–18 for examples of how this can be done for a whole-year programme of study and for an individual study unit.

Construct schemes of work for supplementary units according to guidelines on pages 47–8 of the Order.

Teacher assessment should not be a 'bolt-on' extra at the end. If it is to work properly, bear in mind the attainment targets and the statements of attainment all the time you are planning and teaching the work. They should be explicitly included in your schemes of work.

Pupils must cover eight units in nine terms, so in one of the three years, two units instead of three can be covered. Before deciding which, consider:

1 Y9 pupils will be involved towards the end of the year with SATs for core and foundation subjects. Their burden may be lightened during Y9 by choosing to do only two units.

2 Y7 pupils just transferred from primary school may be given the chance to settle gradually into a different way of working.

3 Time can be gained by combining 'Medieval Realms' with another unit and teaching them both together. An obvious example is 'Castles and Cathedrals', but 'Relations between England and Scotland' or 'Culture and Society in Ireland' or a local study might also be used in this way.

4 Some units might be studied partly in one year and partly in the next. The Scottish and Irish units just mentioned might neatly straddle Y7 and Y8, for example. So might a local study, or a category B unit like 'The Reformation and Counter-Reformation in the 16th Century', which would fit seamlessly and meaningfully between 'Medieval Realms' and 'The Making of the UK'.

Putting your plan together

The best place to start from is where you are. There can't be a school in the country in which some aspects of the National Curriculum are not already being taught.

Begin with an audit of what is being done now in each of years 7, 8 and 9. Set this out on a simple grid. Make sure to include any local history that is being done; this could form the basis of a useful supplementary study unit.

Now consider the core study units which *must* be covered in Key Stage 3 and fit these into suitable places on the grid. The British core units and 'The Era of the Second World War' have to be studied in chronological order, at least one in each of years 7, 8 and 9. You can put 'The Roman Empire' in any year, but it would be sensible to put it where it fits coherently into the other work planned. There are chronological arguments for putting it in Y7. In the years 1991–4 pupils will be coming into Key Stage 3 without necessarily having done Key Stage 2. For these pupils 'The Roman Empire' could be tackled as an introduction to National Curriculum history at the beginning of Y7, emphasising the attainment targets and using the rich variety of sources from the Roman period.

With the supplementary units it can be decided which units to teach and what content to put into them. Before doing this, consider how both these things relate chronologically and thematically to the core unit for that year. Chronological progression and change and development through time are assessed in AT1, and a supplementary unit can be very useful in providing the necessary perspectives for this if carefully related to the core material.

Supplementary units might:

- help develop a year course based on a particular theme, e.g. revolutions;

- give teachers a chance to go on following existing good practice including work in local history which could not be easily fitted into the core;

- enable members of the department to use their own interests and expertise;

- let teachers draw on local strengths and facilities such as museums and other sites, canals, industries or farming patterns;

- help teachers to balance the course as a whole in terms of the history of different parts of the world.

The supplementary units given on pages 47–8 of the Order are just examples. One of these could be chosen, and since publishers are likely to produce books on these subjects, shortage of planning time or of staff may incline schools to follow this course. But school-designed units may well suit a school, its staff and its environment better than the ready-made variety.

Figure 2 shows one school's complete programme of study for Y7 and its detailed scheme of work for the core unit on 'Medieval Realms'.

The matrix in Figure 3 was used as the basis for departmental discussion for a supplementary unit on 'Castles'. It provides a tentative check-list. Other headings might be added, e.g. cross-curricular links. Once completed it might become a teaching plan and a useful statement to explain what is being done. Once the work has been taught it would remain useful as a record and as the basis for review.

HUMANITIES FACULTY SYLLABUS SUMMARY
1991 – 92

Subject: History
Grouping format: Mixed ability
Any special notes:

Year: 7
Approx. no. in each class: 25

CONTENT	OBJECTIVES/SKILLS		MAIN TEACHING METHODS
National Curriculum Core Study Unit 1 – 'The Roman Empire'			Each study unit will include flexible learning. Various active learning exercises, particularly in the form of simulations, have been built into 'Medieval Realms'. (Simulations are also available for 'The Roman Empire'.)
1. Roman expansion	1. AT1	AT2	Resource – based learning will also be integral to these programmes of study, both in the 'classroom' and for homework.
2. Republican + Imperial Rome	2. AT1	AT2	Micro-computers will be used on various occasions, particularly desk-top publishing packages – e.g. homework exercise on Julius Caesar, Magna Carta, the Black Death, Peasants' Revolt, etc.
3. The provinces	3. AT1	AT3	Wide variety of video materials are also available. To be used by staff as and where they feel it to be appropriate.
4. Economy of Roman Britain	4. AT1	AT2 AT3	Didactic teaching, standard textbooks, audio-visual resources, etc. will also be employed.
5. Trade + communications	5. AT1	AT3	
6. Engineering	6. AT1	AT2 AT3	
7. Roman way of life	7. AT1	AT2 AT3	
National Curriculum Core Study Unit 2 – 'Medieval Realms'			
1. Norman Invasion	1. AT1	AT3	
2. Castles	2. AT1	AT3	
3. Feudal System	3. AT1	AT2 AT3	
4. Magna Carta	4. AT1	AT2 AT3	
5. The Church	5. AT1	AT2 AT3	
6. Henry II + Becket	6. AT1	AT2	
7. Village Economy	7. AT1	AT2	
8. Towns + Trade	8. AT1	AT3	
9. Black Death	9. AT1	AT2 AT3	
10. Peasants' Revolt	10. AT1	AT2	
11. England and – Wales, Scotland + Ireland	11. AT1	AT2	
12. Wars of the Roses	12. AT1	AT2 AT3	

PROVISION MADE FOR RANGE OF ABILITY	ASSIGNMENTS, PROJECTS, HOMEWORK	MARKING, RECORDING and ASSESSMENT
Individual work set in some specific circumstances/for specific purposes. Aim to foster and encourage peer-group support and group co-operation.	Getting into the habit of well-presented, well-researched and carefully thought out regular homework. (Homework is usually one item per week, occasionally a homework exercise may extend over two weeks.) Staff and pupils follow same homework exercises/tasks; these are built into pos.	Teacher mark-book and comments on pupils' work. Work is marked in accordance with Lower School Humanities profile (in order to integrate with records of achievement). Pupils to make use of profiles in recording achievement.

Figure 2b Scheme of work for 'Medieval Realms'.

Scheme of work: 'Medieval Realms': Britain c. 1066 – c. 1500' (40 lessons – 20 weeks).

No. of lessons	Topic	Content detail	Resources	Concepts and skills	ATs	Homework	Cross-curricular
3	The Norman Invasion	1. Establish various claims to throne. 2. Events surrounding invasion, including Stamford Bridge and Seulac Hill. 3. Bayeux tapestry – its value. 4. Problems of conquest and consolidation. 5. Norman culture – language, clothing, hairstyles, social organisation and structure.	Outline map of Britain. In Search of History (Aylett), pp. 6 – 9. History of Britain Book 1, pp. 74 – 77. Presenting the Past Book 1, pp. 69 – 77. The Middle Ages (Sauvain) pp. 4 – 7.	Invasion Conquest Normans Saxons Resistance Culture Military power Bayeux tapestry Mapwork, chronology Causation Decision-making	1 2 3	People with a claim to the English throne in 1066 (AT2) Normans win at Hastings – William conquers! (AT1)	Economic Communication Problem-solving IT Multi-cultural Citizenship
3	Castles	1. Why were castles built by the Normans? 2. Siting castles. 3. Basic planning/design. 4. Visible imposition of Norman rule, means of holding the country and rewarding loyal Norman followers.	In Search of History, pp. 12 – 15. Presenting the Past, pp. 78, 79. Video. The Middle Ages, pp. 8 – 13.	National feeling/ identity Saxons Normans Defence Loyalty Reward Cultural transference /mobility Evidence Comparison Decision-making	1 3	William holds power in England (AT1) Siting a castle (AT1)	Economic Communication Problem-solving Personal and social
3	The Feudal System	1. Diagram of feudal system. 2. Rights and responsibilities under the feudal system. 3. Workings of the feudal system.	In Search of History, pp. 10 – 11. Presenting the Past pp. 80 – 82. Departmental sheets – 'feudalism'.	Feudalism Lord Peasant Law Rights/responsibility Taxes and tithes Interdependence Diagrammatic Continuation and change Similarity and difference Decision-making	1 2 3	Feudalism: a good system of organisation? (For whom and why?) (AT2) Women in Medieval Times (AT3)	Citizenship Economic Communication Study Problem-solving Equal opportunities

Figure 2b *continued*

No. of lessons	Topic	Content detail	Resources	Concepts and skills	ATs	Homework	Cross-curricular
5	The Village Economy	1. Description and plan of medieval village and open fields. 2. Central role of agriculture – employment, economy, survival, basis of society/social structure. 3. Domesday Book. Why it was drawn up. Value as a source. 4. Lives of villagers, labour, seasonal round, etc.	Greenleigh – a medieval village (Spartacus). (Activity based pack.) In Search of History, pp. 16 – 17. Ploughing simulation In Search of History, pp. 18 – 21. The Middle Ages, pp. 14 – 23. Greenleigh character cards.	Feudalism Co-operation Census Social structure Community Similarity and difference Continuity and change Empathy Decision-making	1 2	Life in Norman Britain through the eyes of . . . (AT1) The Peasant's Home (AT1)	Economic Environmental Citizenship Communication Numeracy Problem-solving Equal opportunities
3	The power and influence of the Church	1. Clarification of concept of the Church. 2. Role of the Pope and his power. 3. Religious belief. 4. Work of the Church. 5. Monastic orders. 6. Pilgrimage and pilgrims. 7. Church – laity rivalry.	Departmental sheets on Church in Middle Ages. In Search of History, pp. 24 – 28. Video. The Middle Ages, pp. 24 – 29, 38 – 41.	Faith Judgement Good/evil Saint Relics Shrine Monks/nuns Pilgrims Laity Purgatory Opinion Empathy Comparison Change and continuity	1 2 3	Pilgrimage (AT1) The Monastic Life (AT3)	Economic Citizenship Health Communication Personal and social IT
2	Magna Carta	1. Problems inherited by John, e.g. high taxation due to Richard's involvement in Crusades. 2. John's dealings with nobility. 3. Rebellion of nobility. 4. Challenge to monarchy/status quo. 5. Importance re. early rights.	In Search of History, pp. 38 – 39. The Middle Ages, pp. 31 – 32.	Monarchy Nobility Rebellion Duty, rights and justice Compromise Causation Continuity and change	1 2 3	Magna Carta (AT1)	Citizenship Economic Communication IT

No. of lessons	Topic	Content detail	Resources	Concepts and skills	ATs	Homework	Cross-curricular
2	Henry II and Becket	1. Henry brings nobles to heel. 2. Henry and the Church. 3. Becket's opposition to Henry and his subsequent fate.	In Search of History, pp. 30 – 32. The Middle Ages, pp. 30 – 31.	Power struggle Interest groups Monarchy Laity Decision-making Empathy Similarity and difference Causation Continuity and change	1 2	Who did what and why? (AT2)	Citizenship Economic Communication Problem-solving
4	Towns and Trade	1. Geographical extent of Medieval trade. 2. Main communities. 3. Trade fairs and markets. 4. Town markets – basic goods. 5. Trade/craft guilds. 6 Town charters. 7. Growth of towns (as linked to certain functions and/or commodities).	Outline map of Europe. In Search of History, pp. 52 – 59. The Middle Ages, pp. 52 – 59.	Trade/commerce Imports/exports Surplus Urban growth Mobility of ideas Drawing Causation Change and continuity Mapping	1 3	Medieval Trade (AT1) Craft Guilds (AT2)	Economic Environmental Careers(?) Health Communication IT
4	The Black Death	1. Cause, route + manifestation. 2. Spread of plague within England. 3. Cures + preventions 4. Results, ie. reductions of population and labour shortage.	Plague simulation. Video. In Search of History, pp. 44 – 47. Department sheets – Results of Black Death. Middle Ages, pp. 68 – 69. The Black Death (Longman).	Transmission Disease Cults Prevention Discussion Decision-making Empathy Cause and consequence	1 2 3	Medieval Health and Disease (AT1)	Health Economic Communication Study IT Personal and social Numeracy
3	The Peasants' Revolt	1. Causes of revolt. 2. Wat Tyler and the march on London. 3. Richard's response and the defeat of the Revolt. 4. Consequences.	In Search of History, pp. 48 – 51. The Middle Ages, pp. 69 – 71. The Peasants' Revolt (Longman). Video.	Power Revolt Rights Injustice Oppression Justification Causation Change and continuity Empathy	1 2	"Read all about it!" (AT2)	Citizenship Economic IT Communication Study

No. of lessons	Topic	Content detail	Resources	Concepts and skills	ATs	Homework	Cross-curricular
2	Relations between England and Scotland, Ireland and Wales England and Wales	1. Llewellyn the Great and Llewellyn ap Gruffud. The rise of Gwynedd. 2. Llewellyn's refusal to pay homage. 3. Edward's invasion of Wales. 4. Results – new Welsh regions. 5. Owen Glyndwr – the challenge to English authority and its failure.	In Search of History, pp. 40 – 41. Department sheets. The Middle Ages pp. 46 – 47.	Nation and nationalism Invasion Control Revolt Resistance Power and power struggles Political expansion Hegemony Identity Mapwork	1 2	The way i see it.... (AT2)	Citizenship Communication IT Problem-solving
2	England and Scotland	1. Edward I's designs on Scotland. John Balliol. 2. Edward invades. Wallace. 3. Robert Bruce. 4. Battle of Bannock Burn. 5. Continued unrest (→ 1707).	In Search of History, pp. 40 – 41. Department sheets. The Middle Ages, pp. 48 – 49.	Concepts and skills as listed above	1 2		Citizenship Communication Problem-solving IT Health
2	England and Ireland	1. The Normans and Ireland. de Clare. 2. Conquerors → Irish landlords. 3. Edward I and the Bruces.	Department sheets.	As above	1 2	Sort it out! (AT1)	Citizenship IT Communication Problem-solving
2	The Wars of the Roses	1. Rivalry between Houses of York and Lancaster. 2. Outline of events. 3. Resolution – battle of Bosworth and marriage of Henry and Elizabeth.	In Search of History, pp. 82 – 83. The Middle Ages, p. 75.	Royal houses Civil war Reconciliation Causation Diagrammatic Continuity and change	1 2 3	Medieval costume (AT3) Summary timeline of Medieval England (AT1)	Communication Study

Figure 3 *Departmental discussion plan for a supplementary unit.*

HSU Title: 'CASTLES'

Attainment targets	Content	Key concepts	Resources	Learning experiences	Assessment	Outcome/ future developments
AT1 AT2 AT3	Introduction: Variety of castles.	Power	Pictures.	Sorting exercise: styles, materials, ages, locations.		
	William I and Norman castles.	Military Political Government	Bayeux Tapestry. Maps. X.ref. to 'Medieval Realms' material. Simulation materials.	Normans and castles – consideration of attitudes, values. Siting exercise.		
	Changes in castle design – technological 'arms race'. Attack and defence.	Style Prestige Technology	Sources – pictures and written.	Sequencing and explanation.	AT1 – Timing of changes and the causes of change.	
	Building castles. Techniques. Lives of workers.	Style Technology	Sources on Medieval building (general) and material on Welsh Edwardian castles.	Understanding problems, limits and scope of building techniques. Problem-solving. Similarity and difference with modern building.		
	Life in a castle. Castle as home; community. Lives of women, children, servants.	Household Community Retainer	Wall-chart, sources and visit.	Consideration of values, life-style. Site – recording and evaulation.	AT3 – Site report	
	Decline of castles. Castles in 15th and 16th centuries.	Technology Parliament Standard of living	Different explanations of decline of castles. Pictures. X-ref. to 'Medieval Realms'.	Comparison of secondary sources in context.	AT2 – Finding sources to support or contradict given accounts.	

2 PLANNING FOR ASSESSMENT

Introduction Most teachers see assessment and how to carry it out as the major burden facing them in relation to the delivery of the National Curriculum. Management considerations tend to dominate discussion and there is widespread concern about complexity and over-assessment.

Most of this stems from the assessment environment which we have inherited from the past. We hear a great deal about assessment being an integral part of teaching and learning, and this tends to be one of those slogans that it is all too easy to agree with but not implement in practice. What indeed does it mean in practice?

Trevor Rogers, in an article on coursework and continuous assessment, draws an analogy with a missile which, when homing in on its target, does not necessarily move along the path initially planned for it.[1] Its course is constantly modified by information which it provides to its controllers. The missile in turn receives information upon which it acts. The nature of this model, with its stress upon continuity, feedback and partnership, is central to the integration of assessment with teaching and learning. It is, however, not one with which the majority of teachers and students, particularly in secondary schools, have been familiar. Their past experience has been dominated by formal, timed, largely end-of-course tests upon which student performance has been evaluated by means of marks and grades. These tell us very little about learning and achievement, but make it easy to compare students with one another. Assessment for the National Curriculum, on the other hand, if it is to work well for everyone, requires a very different environment: one which is more akin to Rogers's model. In educational terms, it is one in which evidence of success can be demonstrated through a broad range of activities carried out in a variety of contexts: in which there is a major emphasis upon identifying progress through a range of levels and in which student performance is compared and

1   H G Macintosh ed; *Techniques and Problems of Assessment: A Practical Handbook for Teachers*, E J Arnold, 1974

described against publicly stated objectives – in this case attainment targets and statements of attainment.

At a practical level, achieving ends such as these will require changes in the range of activities promoted in the classroom, in the kind of questions and tasks given to pupils and in the ways pupils' work is evaluated and recorded. The previous sentence has deliberately not referred to activities such as marking, setting and reporting. This is because if there is a continuation of much past practice in these areas, time which no one can afford will be wasted and assessment will not be used in ways which can help progress and enhance quality in the classroom. Generalities are of little use, however, unless they can be translated into the practice of day-to-day classroom management. This will be the task of the rest of this chapter.

Managing assessment

Successful management, here as anywhere else, requires detailed knowledge of the relevant material – in this case of the National Curriculum requirements for history and related subjects – and taking carefully considered decisions which are then worked through and evaluated.

The key decisions which need to be taken can be approached via five questions. These questions are obviously interrelated, but each focuses upon a particular issue.

What do I want to assess? Clearly there are very many possible answers to this question. I may wish to determine the knowledge and understanding students have gained during a lesson, over a term or at the end of a course. The focus may be as wide as the First World War, or as limited as the Sarajevo assassination. Assessment may be restricted to the recall of information or to the analyis of photographic evidence. It may be sufficient for me merely to know whether or not something has been grasped; or I may need to know not just if, but how well it has been grasped.

What knowledge, skills and understanding will pupils need to possess in order to make a response? Within AT3 of the National Curriculum, for instance, level 3 requires pupils to demonstrate the ability to make deductions from historical sources. The example given is to arrive at decisions about social groups in Victorian Britain by looking at the clothes people wore. How well pupils are going to be able to respond to this depends crucially upon the knowledge they already have, and upon their ability to relate the familiar to the unfamiliar. Imagine trying to deduce anything at all from the clothing of beings who were totally alien. At the very least pupils will need to know about what jobs people did and about the relative cost of different sorts of clothing materials.

What kind of questions or tasks will I need to set in order for pupils' responses to provide reliable evidence of achievement? A poorly designed multiple choice test, for example, in which all the pupils give the correct answer because the alternatives are so implausible, does not constitute reliable evidence of knowledge. Similarly, if the intention is to assess pupils' understanding of causation, the problem which they are given must not be one that can be tackled successfully solely by producing information in an unstructured way. Questions which have to do with 'why?' should not be capable of being satisfactorily answered by answers which deal only with 'what?'.

What sort of responses do I expect questions to elicit?
Some questions are simple in the sense of being hit or miss. Evaluating responses to such single-target questions where answers are either correct or incorrect has a degree of certainty about it which is reassuring. But they provide only limited information about pupils' present attainments, and little guidance to aid future progress. More enlightening about pupils' ability to handle the complexities of the historical record are questions capable of producing answers falling not merely into two categories – right and wrong – but into a range of responses. Criteria for distinguishing these responses have to be established. 'Correctness' needs to be identified in terms, for example, of pupils' ability to use an increasingly wide frame of reference or to employ sources with greater degrees of sophistication. Equally important are decisions about how responses are to be made. Are written answers necessarily more appropriate and reliable than oral answers? If responses are to be oral, do they have to result from formal testing or from, say, observation of group discussion?

How do I record results in ways which will help teaching and learning, inform pupils and facilitate reporting? The model for assessment which is suggested in the following pages is designed to meet these three purposes and to manage more effectively what can be a most time-consuming activity. It is intended to replace existing procedures for the awarding of marks and grades, with an approach which is closer to the demands of the National Curriculum.

Rationale Some decisions about what is to be assessed have been taken nationally and are spelt out in the programmes of study, attainment targets and statements of attainment for history. But the National Curriculum is not intended to be a teaching syllabus; nor does it attempt to chart the whole of children's learning in history over eleven years. What it does is identify those aspects of performance which are to be assessed and reported upon – and leave to the teacher the essential responsibility of ensuring that the process and the results of assessment are used to enhance teaching and to improve learning. As with grades or marks, statements of attainment cannot by themselves convey sufficient information to be of much help in those tasks.

A limitation which is built into most statements of achievement or grade descriptions is that they say little about the kind of activity that had to be undertaken by the pupil to get there. Often they have, perforce, to be framed at a level of generality which makes them capable of wide application in a variety of circumstances. As a consequence, a statement such as 'Mary can evaluate written against non-written sources' is limited in the value it has. It tells us nothing, for example, about how difficult the sources might have been or about what Mary actually had to do. Indicating not merely the nature of the sources (written and non-written) but also any linguistic or conceptual problems they might have posed would be a more certain pointer to the level of Mary's achievement. Similarly, it would be useful to know something about the particular task, or tasks, that Mary did and how she responded. Information of this kind is valuable both in reporting what has been done already and as a guide to ways in which progress might be made. Introducing qualifications – 'simple sources', 'complex processes' – into statements or descriptions helps, but only so far.

Tracking pupils' achievements

The model of assessment and recording which is proposed here offers a way of incorporating the attainment targets and levels of attainment described in the National Curriculum within the activities of teaching, learning and assessment. It is not intended to be rigid. For example, it is shown as identifying pupils' attainment by presenting information about four aspects of their performance; but there is no reason why more could not be included – the amount of time taken, say, or the level of language used in the response. It is important also to stress that the examples given of the model are illustrative. They do not preclude the need to make decisions and exercise judgement about what is to be recorded and how often.

The basic framework of the model is shown in Figure 4. This presents information about pupils' performance along four dimensions: Task,

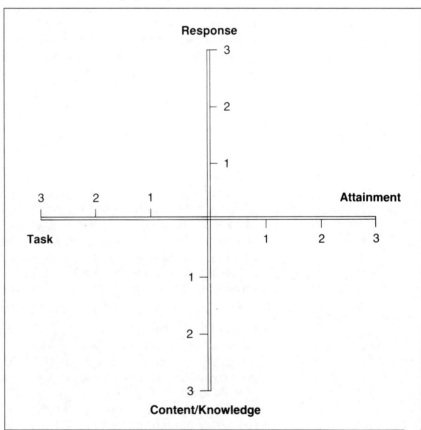

Figure 4 *Four-dimensional framework for assessment and recording.*

Response, Attainment, and Content/Knowledge. For those who find acronyms helpful the strategy could be described as one of TRACKing.

- TASK: what it is the pupil does.

- RESPONSE: the way in which the pupil copes with the task.

- ATTAINMENT: what is assessed – the attainment target(s) and level(s).

- CONTENT/KNOWLEDGE: the kind of historical information, conceptual understanding or skill the pupil is able to use.

In Figure 4 each of the four dimensions is shown as having three ascending levels of difficulty, with 3 representing the highest level. But clearly, as shown in some of the later examples, there is a degree of flexibility. The number of levels may be varied. Or, instead of being hierarchically ordered, one or more of the dimensions may show different kinds of activity all of which are on a par as far as difficulty goes. This can be represented diagrammatically by a single rather than a double line. Other variations will no doubt occur to you.

Using this framework it is possible, with reasonable economy, both to plan for assessment and to build up an informative picture of how individual pupils are faring – as the examples which follow attempt to demonstrate. According to particular needs, it can be a vehicle for showing how pupils perform on one activity or on a number of activities; their achievements in relation to one attainment target or to several; over the course of a week, a term or the whole of the key stage. Most importantly, it offers the possibility of indicating the setting within which a pupil registers the achievement. By placing attainment targets and levels in a context, and by representing achievement in this way, the model also makes it easier to share the results of assessment with pupils – and thereby to encourage improvement.

The four examples which follow demonstrate different approaches to planning for and recording the results of assessing pupils' historical ability in National Curriculum terms:

1 Plots achievements in one strand across three levels of attainment – the levels are hierarchical.

2 Plots achievements in the various strands within one level – in this case the levels are not hierarchical; but it is assumed that teachers will wish to encourage pupils to move beyond the minimum required to demonstrate achievement of the level. The example, therefore, suggests directions in which possible responses might be extended.

3 Focuses upon one strand at one level. As with example 2 it suggests ways in which pupils' responses might look further than that which is minimally demanded. It also indicates a means of plotting achievements which fall below a given level but which mark an advance upon the preceding one.

4 Considers achievements across three levels of an unstranded attainment target.

Example 1 The first example (Figure 5) is concerned with achievements at the first three levels of one strand in AT1 – knowledge and understanding of history. It would represent, therefore, a major aspect of pupils' performance throughout the whole of the first key stage.

To take each dimension in turn:

T: Identifies the number of variables with which pupils are able to cope – the number of items in a story; the number of objects; or the number of changes.

R: Indicates two levels of response – the ability to put forward a valid sequence, of events or objects, or a valid set of changes; and, at a higher level of difficulty, the ability to offer more than one valid sequence or set. Thus, for example, a pupil might be able to sequence family photographs both according to generation – self, father, grandfather – and to the date at which they were taken, when that produces a different sequence.

A: The three levels within the attainment target strand are: place in sequence events in a story about the past; place familiar objects in chronological order; describe changes over a period of time.

C/K: Shows the extent to which the pupil is able to tackle activities unaided. Clearly all pupils need some guidance and explanation; but what is recorded along this dimension is the teacher's judgement about the extent to which a pupil operates without support.

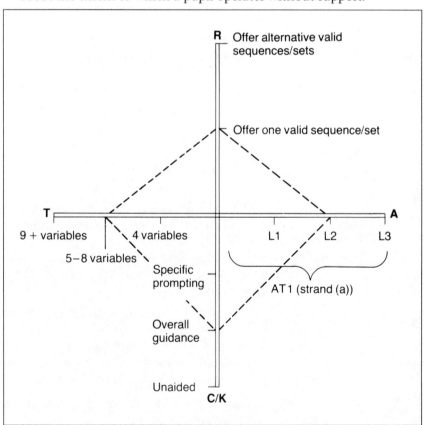

Figure 5 Assessment and recording framework for three levels of one strand in AT1.

As an example, the broken line tracks the performance of a pupil who, with a little help, is able to place five photographs of her family in a valid chronological sequence. It may represent her achievement at the end of Key Stage 1, or part way through. It may be retained in this form, or further (perhaps differently coloured) lines may be added later to indicate where her performance has improved.

Example 2 There are a number of strands running through AT1. The second example (Figure 6) suggests a way of managing this, of plotting what pupils do in different strands within the one level – here it is level 4. In this case the attainment dimension is not hierarchical. All three strands are at the same level of difficulty, and this is shown by the single line. It assumes that pupils undertake at least three different activities or assignments, each targeted on a given strand.

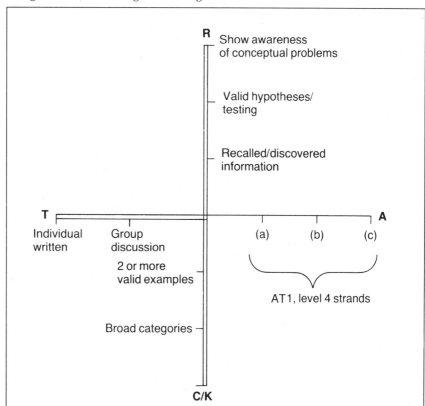

Figure 6 Assessment and recording framework for several strands in AT1, level 4.

Again, to consider each of the dimensions:

T: There are two levels of task: to contribute to a small group discussion on an appropriate topic; and to undertake a piece of individual written work. The first of these poses obvious assessment problems for the teacher. It demands quick observation and careful judgement. But, with the right structure, activity of this kind can yield evidence of pupils' abilities which may not otherwise emerge.

R: Three possible kinds of response are indicated:

- those based on information recalled or discovered in reference material;

- those which in addition suggest valid hypotheses and ways of testing them (one consequence of the Black Death may have been an emphasis on public hygiene – how can we find out?);

- those which recognise some of the conceptual problems involved ('change or not change' may lie in the degree of detail given in the description – children went to school 100 years ago, but going to school today is a different experience; people in the 14th century had a different set of 'causes' for the Black Death; the 'features' of an historical situation may be grouped into different sorts of categories).

The last two levels are difficult. Few may reach them. But they do represent extensions of the National Curriculum level which some may be encouraged to explore.

A: The three strands at level 4 are:

- recognise that over time some things changed and others stayed the same;

- show an awareness that historical events usually have more than one cause and consequence:

- describe different features of an historical period.

C/K: This dimension indicates those pupils who:

- show a sufficient grasp of content to give at least two valid examples in each of the categories (change and similarity over 100 years; cause and consequence of one event; different features of a situation);

- on the basis of recalled or discovered information are able to cope with broader categories (longer than 100 years; more than one event or situation).

This example assumes that pupils are achieving at least the minimum required to reach level 4 in each of the strands. They are, for instance, able to give the requisite number of appropriate examples. And some can do much more. By extending the C/K dimension, however, it would be possible also to record the attainment of pupils who had not yet quite done enough – who, for instance, gave valid but too few examples.

Example 3 This example focuses upon one strand (strand (b)) at one level (level 7) in AT1 – 'show how the different causes of an historical event are connected'. It is concerned with recording how well pupils fared in tackling an exercise aimed specifically at this statement of attainment.

The exercise required pupils to consider the causes of the First World War and how they were linked. As illustrated in Figure 7, pupils were given two statements which identified significant end-points: 'Germany declares war on Russia' and 'Britain declares war on Germany'.

Figure 8 shows what they then had to do and the criteria against which their responses were assessed and recorded.

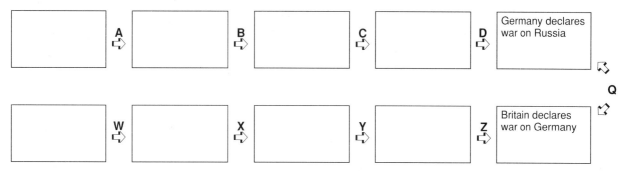

Figure 7 *Causes of the First World War.*

T: Pupils had three tasks:

- to select, for each statement, four issues or events leading up to this end-point and present them in logical or chronological order;

- to describe, in each case, the links both between the items selected and with the end-point;

- to explain how the two given statements were linked.

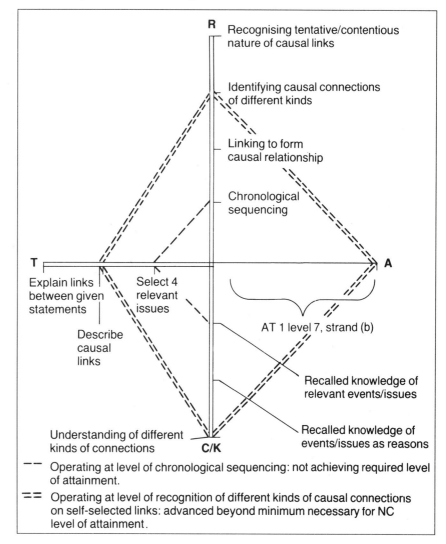

Figure 8 *Assessment and recording framework for AT1, level 7.*

The tasks were considered to be in ascending order of difficulty in terms of the increasingly complex ways in which pupils had to organise issues and events.

R: Responses required pupils to be able to describe issues and events succinctly and to write in extended prose. The hierarchical elements of this dimension were:

- place issues or events in chronological sequence;

- link selected issues and events before the First World War together to create a causal relationship;

- identify causal connections of different kinds (e.g. (a) *cause and effect* – the assassination of Franz Ferdinand and the Austrian ultimatum; (b) *two events connected by a third* – the German declaration of war on Russia and the British declaration of war on Germany linked by the existence of the Franco-Russian and Anglo-French agreements);

- show how connections are not inevitable but often tentative and contentious (e.g. the existence of two armed camps may be variously put forward as a reason for the outbreak of war or for the maintenance of peace).

Two points about these response levels:

- As the level within the National Curriculum requires, they focus upon the ability to make connections between events and issues in order to provide an explanation.

- The first of the response levels does not meet the National Curriculum description – the third and fourth are extensions of it. The first sees that items in the story may be linked in time, but not how they can be joined together to become causes and take on explanatory power. Pupils need only achieve the second level, but reaching for the third and fourth helps them move towards the next of the National Curriculum goals.

A:

- show how the different causes of an historical event are connected (AT1b, level 7).

C/K:

- recalled knowledge of events and issues during the years before the First World War;

- recalled knowledge of the way events and issues have been seen as reasons for the various declarations of war;

- an understanding of different kinds of connections.

Example 4 This final example (Figure 9) focuses on the higher levels of AT3 – the use of historical sources.

T: It assumes that the pupils' task (perhaps as an extended coursework assignment) is to consider the way in which East–West relations during the five years following the Second World War were portrayed in the contemporary British media. In particular, and in order of difficulty, it is to:

- identify the point of view intended to be conveyed by one selected newsreel report;

- suggest reasons for differences in the interpretation of events between various sections of the media and at different times during the five years;

- use the sources to produce a commentary on a recent textbook account of some aspect of relations during that time.

R: The response required is the ability to write in extended prose form. With coursework especially it may also be necessary to judge between those pupils who: require specific prompts; are able to work effectively given overall guidance; and are able to create their own structure within which to work. Hierarchically pupils should:

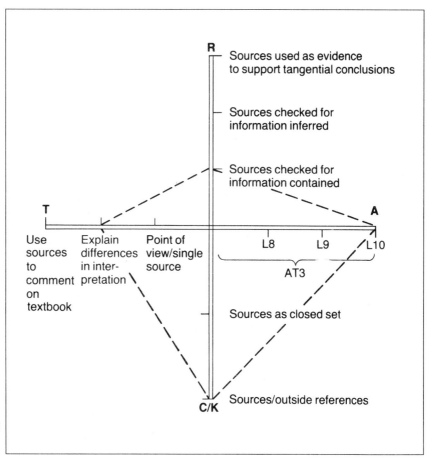

Figure 9   Assessment and recording framework for AT3, levels 8–10.

- recognise that sources give information which may be useful, can be checked for accuracy and is necessarily incomplete;

- recognise that sources provide, wittingly or unwittingly, information which may be inferred on the basis of knowledge of the period and of issues and events;

- recognise that sources may be used as evidence for supporting statements which may be tangential to the subject of the source (e.g. newsreels on the Berlin crisis as evidence of British public opinion).

A: The levels (8–10) within the attainment target are:

- show how a source which is unreliable can nevertheless be useful;

- show an understanding that a source can be more or less valuable depending on the questions asked of it;

- explain the problematic nature of historical evidence, showing an awareness that judgements based on historical sources may well be provisional.

C/K: Given the nature of this assignment, the emphasis is upon abilities such as cross-referencing between sources both of the same and of different kinds, and beween sources and knowledge of events; the erection and testing of hypotheses; and an understanding of the nature – the strengths and limitations – of contemporary media sources.

Within this two levels are assumed:

- sources given seen as a closed set (i.e. little or no reference to material/knowledge outside them);

- sources and outside references seen as mutually supportive (i.e. understanding of sources informed by references and vice versa).

The dotted line shows, as an example, the performance of a student who is able to explain differences in the interpretation of events given in the sources by reference to the differing information they contain and to explain the limitations of the sources by referring to information given outside the sources.

Conclusion

What in summary are the potential benefits of using such a model?

1 It can be used to indicate performances either upon a single piece of work or upon several pieces over a period of time; at a single level or over a range of levels.

2 It is relatively simple and not unduly time-consuming; for example, it avoids the need for lengthy prose.

3 It presents the results of assessment in ways which can be readily shared with pupils and hence helps them to become involved in the assessment of their own performance.

4 Above all, it facilitates the crucial link between planning the 'what' and 'how' of assessment, and recording and reporting its results.

3 TEACHING AND ASSESSING

Teaching at Key Stage 1

The demands of the National Curriculum have placed all teachers under great pressure, but those working at Key Stage 1 have a particular worry. They are responsible for teaching the rudiments of reading, writing and arithmetic, which some pupils will not have sufficiently mastered when they leave Key Stage 1. How can they meet the needs of National Curriculum history while at the same time acquiring the fundamental skills? Fortunately history interlinks naturally with many other subjects, so that with careful planning and monitoring it can be introduced at this early stage.

Teaching history at this stage must be visual and 'hands on'. It needs to come from the pupils' experiences so that they can relate to it and feel a sense of the past.

Reception pupils

1 Many pupils like to talk about what they have done at home or at the weekend. The concept of the past comes from them: 'Yesterday we went to . . .' or 'We did . . . yesterday.' Ask them: 'What did you do yesterday?' or 'What did we do at school yesterday?' They could draw a picture and write a sentence or two about what they did.

2 Talk about the days of the week. 'What day was yesterday?' 'What day is it today?' 'What day will it be tomorrow?' Make 'days of the week' cards. Ask the more able to put them in the right order or put them on the wall with movable signs of 'yesterday', 'today' and 'tomorrow' which can be transferred to the correct days:

Sunday Monday Tuesday Wednesday Thursday Friday Saturday

3 Have a classroom calendar on which pupils can cross off yesterday's day and on which the teacher can write important events, including historical ones such as Bonfire Night or important religious days in Christianity, Islam or other faiths.

4 Make a class or wall diary so that pupils can see what has happened in their lives. Do it at a time when there is much happening, such as birthdays or a major school or class event in which many of them are involved.

5 Use the pupils' own history as a starting point. If possible, get them to bring in photographs of themselves when they were younger. Talk about how they have changed physically. Discuss what they can do now that they couldn't do in the past. Ask them to put their photos on a time scale from 0 to 5 years:

| to 1 yr | 1 to 2 yrs | 2 to 3 yrs | 3 to 4 yrs | 4 to 5yrs |

6 An extension of days of the week is to talk about seasons and months. 'What was the last month?' 'What was the last season we had?' 'How do you know it was that season?' 'What was last year if this year is 199_?' The pupils could draw pictures of what they did last season or month, especially if it was something memorable such as Christmas, Purim, Ramadan or their birthday.

7 Introduce the idea of one event happening after another and one event leading on to another, by telling stories which the pupils know and can join in retelling, such as 'Cinderella', 'Little Red Riding Hood', 'The Three Bears' and 'The Three Little Pigs'. Get them to draw three pictures telling a story they have heard. The first one may be of Little Red Riding Hood walking in the forest and meeting the wolf, the second one may be of the wolf dressed up as Grandmother, and the third may be of the woodcutter rescuing Grandmother and/or Red Riding Hood. The pupils can tell the story to the class in their own words using their drawings to help them. Another way to help them with sequencing is to get them to put several pictures in the correct order in which the events happened.

8 Introduce the idea that the past was different in various significant ways from the present by telling stories which begin 'Once upon a time', 'Long, long ago' or 'Many years ago'; and after they have heard them, discuss what the people wore, how they lived and what it must have been like in those days. Use well-known historical stories such as 'Robin Hood' or 'Dick Whittington'. Ask questions about the stories which get the pupils to think about how people lived in those days:
'Why did Dick Whittington walk to London?' 'What might he have seen along the way?' 'Would he have seen the same things as we see today?' 'Why was Robin Hood so called?' 'Why didn't he use a gun instead of a bow and arrow?'

Year 1 and year 2 pupils The approach to history in these two years will depend on what has been taught in the reception class. It is highly likely that the teacher will have to go over what has already been taught. A great deal of Key Stage 1 teaching needs repetition and revision so that the pupils have thoroughly understood what they have learnt.

1 Use assemblies for telling pupils about people who lived in the past. These could be biblical characters such as Moses who was found in the bulrushes or Joseph and his coat of many colours. Jesus might play an important part – from his birth to his life as a boy and a man. Show the pupils pictures to go with the stories so that pupils get an idea of how people lived and what they wore. Stories about famous saints could also be told, especially on their saint days. Encourage the pupils to think why they were made saints. Use examples from other religions in the same way: Guru Gobind Singh; Wesak and the birth of Buddha; Purim and the story of Esther.

Use assemblies also for thinking about people who have helped us with what they have invented (e.g. Alexander Graham Bell and the telephone or Marie Curie and radium), or with what they have discovered as explorers so that we have a greater understanding of the world.

Follow up the assembly by asking pupils to draw a picture and write about the person they have just been told about, or to pretend that they lived at that time and were helped by or met that famous person. They could find out what happened before that person lived and what has happened since.

2 Link work on religious festivals such as Easter, Passover or Ramadan with assemblies. If possible introduce a variety of religions and cultures, especially if there are pupils from various religions or cultures in the school.

Figure 10 Activities associated with Christmas, Key Stage 1.

A suggested topic plan for activities associated with Christmas with a historical bias is shown in Figure 10.

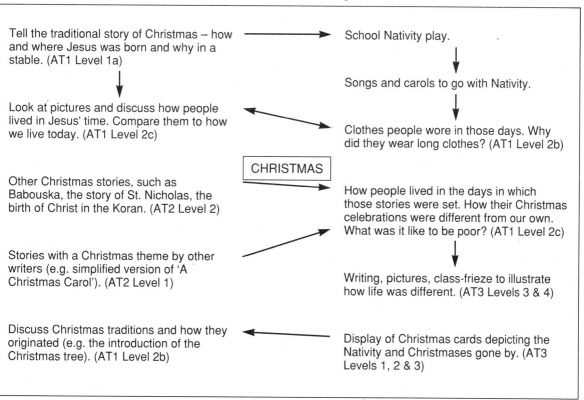

3 Some history teaching will be unplanned. A pupil may have been on a family visit to a place of historical interest or may bring in an object of interest from the past. Encourage the pupil to talk about the visit – what it was like, what was interesting, what was surprising or new. Encourage the rest of the class to ask questions.

Extend this by setting up a history table in the classroom to which the pupils can add. It could be centred on an object brought in or on a visit. A 'castle table', for example, might have a collection of books and pictures to do with castles, perhaps some model knights in armour from home (Lego knights will do!) and some reproductions of implements (such as hammers, chisels, wooden plates) which may have been used in a castle.

4 Another way of teaching history is as a class lesson, especially if the teacher wants to cover a certain aspect. Tell a story about a famous historical person to the pupils and then get them to act it out for themselves. For example, 'Guy Fawkes and the Gunpowder Plot':

'Move quietly around the room so that no one can hear you . . . Pretend to try to move some heavy barrels of gunpowder into the cellars under the Houses of Parliament. You may need some help from a friend . . . Hide the barrels of gunpowder where no one will find them. Where have you put them? Now pretend to be King James's soldiers. How would you move? You have had a 'tip-off' about some hidden gunpowder – make sure you look thoroughly for it. Where do you think it could have been hidden? There! You've found it! What do you do next?'

Discuss afterwards how they felt being in the shoes of Guy Fawkes and the soldiers. Which part would they rather play and why? If possible split the class in two parts – the conspirators and the soldiers.

5 Base your history teaching on a current television programme for children which has a historical bias. Record the programme for future use and review. Use the teachers' handbook as a guide to discussing the programme beforehand and for follow-up lessons. Television is particularly good for teaching history because pupils can see for themselves what life was like in the past. It brings history to life more than pictures can.

6 Another way of making history come alive to pupils is for them to visit a well-known or local historical site, preferably near to school. Castles are especially popular as pupils can clamber round them and see artefacts such as cannons and armour, so that they can visualise how people used to live and why castles were built.

Some points to remember when visiting a historical site:

- Be aware of, and follow, local authority regulations regarding visits.

- Go there yourself before the school visit so that you know where everything is. If possible pick up booklets, posters and postcards for display at school, which you can use in talking about the place to the pupils.

- Make a note of any points to be avoided which may not be of interest to pupils or may be dangerous.

- Make a note of any points of interest which the pupils should not miss.

- Encourage pupils to be observant. Bring pencils and paper so that they can draw something that has interested them, or give them a simple worksheet to fill in. An example of a possible worksheet is shown in Figure 11.

Name _____

Name of the castle _____

Does anyone live in it now? _____

Who used to live in it? _____

Castles were made to keep the enemy out. Find and draw four parts of the castle which could be used to stop the enemy.

Castles were also lived in. Draw part of the castle that was for living in.

What did you like best about the castle you saw?

_____

Figure 11 *Worksheet for an historical site visit, Key Stage 1.*

7 Many teachers prefer a topic-based approach which can be biased towards one curriculum area but with others linked to it. The topic may be the same throughout the school or it may be just for one particular class. Much depends on the resources available. Topics usually do not last for more than a term. They should be planned as much as a year in advance so that teachers have the time to collect materials and plan thoroughly what they intend to do.

Figure 12 offers a suggestion for a year's topic plan which has a history bias.

Year Group	Term 1	Term 2	Term 3
Year 1	Transport	Ourselves/ our family	Sleeping Beauty (or similar story)
Year 2	Celebrations	Change	Our school/ our town

Figure 12 *Topic plan with history bias, Key Stage 1.*

When you have chosen a topic title, make a flow diagram or plan showing how subject areas can be linked together. A brainstorming session with other teachers will produce even more ideas.

The topic plans on 'Change' and 'Sleeping Beauty' in Figures 13 and 14 show how these topics can provide a framework for work aimed at the attainment targets in history and in various other subjects.

History

Changes in children's own lives (from babyhood to starting school). AT1

↓

Photographs of children when they were younger for discussion and comparison. ATs 1,3 ——→ Photographs of parents and grandparents when they were children. Compare and discuss differences in clothes, hair styles, toys, etc. ATs 1, 2, 3 ——→ How children looked further back in time (e.g. in Victorian times) by investigating old photos. ATs 1, 2

↓

Changes in children's families and adults around them. AT1

Photographs of parents, grandparents and other siblings to form a family tree. ATs 1, 3

Have a day/week in school doing exactly what someone did in the past.

Visit from parent and grandparent to talk about how times have changed since they were children. Discuss the differences between the two life-styles. ATs 1, 2, 3

↓

Make a list of the differences. AT 1

If possible have someone who used to attend the school as a child or a teacher so that they can talk about what life was like when they were there. ATs 1, 3

↓

Find out what the differences were 100 years ago. What games did children play? What did they do in their spare time or when they got home from school? AT1 ——→ Class survey of what children would miss most if they lived 100 years ago, knowing what they have now.

CHANGE

Music

Listen to some of the music that was popular when parents and grandparents were children.

↓

Teach some of the catchier songs such as 'When the Red, Red Robin' or 'Yellow Submarine'. (See A. & C. Black's *Ta-ra-ra boom-de-ay* and *Apusskidu* for more ideas.)

Maths

Change of time – chronology. What children did yesterday, are doing today and will be doing tomorrow in written and pictorial form. ATs 1, 9, 12

↓

Telling the time – o'clock, half past, quarter past, hours, minutes, seconds. AT8

↓

Practical work – what can children do in . . . seconds/ . . . minutes? Compare and contrast with others. Record results. ATs 9, 12

Change of number – what happens when you +, −, ÷, and × certain numbers? ATs 2, 3, 5

Graph of what children would like to be when they are grown up. Talk about findings. ATs 12, 13

English

Creative writing on what children would like to turn into if given a magic potion. ATs 3, 4, 5

↑

Make up spells to change . . . into . . . ATs 3, 4, 5

↑

Discussion on work produced. AT1

Reading for further information and enjoyment. AT2

Science

Change of human life cycle. Collect pictures of people of different ages and sort them into groups. ATs 3, 4

Change of colours – by mixing paints to make other colours, adding water to inks on blotting paper to see what happens. AT1

Change of state – hot and cold, melting and freezing; experiments using water, ice, different methods of insulation. ATs 1, 8, 13

Change of weather conditions – daily recording of weather, temperature, etc. on a graph. AT9

Technology

Make and design own clock. ATs 1, 2, 3, 4

Using construction toys and/or recycled materials make a machine which can change . . . into . . .

Change in plant life. Growth – grow your own seeds and note their progress. What do they need to grow? ATs 1, 2

Decay – plant a variety of living things (e.g. apple, leaf) and dead things (e.g. plastic bag, paper) in the ground and after a certain length of time dig them out to see what has happened. ATs 1, 2, 5

Change of seasons (including months of the year) – how does the weather vary for each season? AT9

Figure 13 *Topic plan: 'Change'.*

History

Show pictures and slides of castles – discussion on what they looked like, why they were built, etc. ATs 1, 2

Explain how they were built using slides and pictures; get the children to explain how people lived in them. ATs 1, 3

Visit local castle for children to explore. AT3

Find out what happened to the castle visited over the years, e.g. why it is in ruins or has had parts added. ATs 1, 3

Consider materials used to build castles – how they were made and how long they took to finish. Why they were located at particular sites. AT3

Pictures of castles from other areas for contrast and comparison. ATs 1, 2

Collect 'castle' words – 'dungeon', 'moat', etc.

Find out how people lived in castles.

Different rooms and floors – what they ⟶ What could you find outside the castle? were used for. Map of the castle. Moat, etc.

How castles protected the inhabitants from invaders.

Knights, jousting, Crusades, King Arthur.

SLEEPING BEAUTY

Science/technology

Make own drawbridge using pulleys and levers. ATs 1, 10, 13

Make own moat – what do you need to make it watertight, what can float/sink in it? ATs 1, 6

Use of different materials to see who can make the strongest wall. Do walls have to be built a certain way for strength? ATs 1, 6, 10

Flight – use of catapults, missiles, etc. ATs 1, 6, 10, 13

Day and night – discuss the need for sleep. ATs 2, 3, 13

Hibernation – why do animals hibernate and which ones do? Migration of birds.

Maths

Names and properties of 2-d and 3-d shapes. ATs 1, 8, 9, 10

Make a castle using 3-d shapes. ATs 1, 8, 9, 10

Comparisons of length, size, shape, etc. ATs 1, 9, 10, 12

Graph of how many hours children sleep, what time they get up/go to bed. ATs 3, 4, 9, 12, 13, 14

Tessellations – how shapes fit together. ATs 9, 10, 11, 12

English

Story of Sleeping Beauty – to start topic. ATs 1, 2

Other stories with princesses and castles, e.g. 'Rumpelstiltskin', 'The Princess and the Pea'.

Write a fairy story starting 'Once upon a time' or 'Long, long ago'. ATs 3, 4, 5

Put pictures of Sleeping Beauty in the correct order. Write a sentence or two about each one. ATs 3, 4, 5

Art

Design your own shield or flag.

Make a plan of a castle using boxes for a bird's-eye view.

Design your own castle – modern or old-fashioned.

Make your own knight/armour using tin foil.

Music

'There was a princess long ago' – singing game.
Listen to short excerpts of 'Sleeping Beauty'. Discuss what the children heard with reference to the story.

Drama

Individual and group work on the story of Sleeping Beauty. Act out the story or do excerpts.

Figure 14   Topic plan: 'Sleeping Beauty'

Assessing at Key Stage 1

Assessment is a continuous process – teachers are always gauging their pupils' response to lessons. Have the pupils thoroughly understood or should I go over it again to make sure? Which pupils need more help and which can carry on at their own rate? Did the teaching material meet the needs of all pupils? Now that we are being asked to assess our pupils' progress in relation to the attainment targets in each curriculum area we need to rethink our methods of assessment and to make it more precise, not to begin something quite new.

It is a good idea as a staff to get together to discuss how each teacher has carried out assessment so that ideas can be shared and problems ironed out. Make sure that recording sheets are easy to follow and quick to fill in.

When assessing history several statements of attainment may be met at the same time. Much assessment will be verbal at Key Stage 1 but some recording may be done in the form of drawings or simple written work, such as answering 'yes' or 'no' to questions or pictures. If the pupil has done any form of recording, keep it as an example of work and use it to compare with future progress.

Attainment targets and classroom activities

The following table sets out against each statement of attainment an example of a classroom activity in which it might be reached. For convenience, the progressive stages of each of the different abilities involved are listed consecutively.

AT1 – knowledge and understanding of history The development of the ability to describe and explain historical change and cause, and analyse different features of historical situations.

Level	Statements of attainment (Order, page 3)	Classroom activities
1a	place in sequence events in a story about the past.	putting pictures from an historical story in the correct order; retelling the story to the teacher; drawing a series of pictures telling the story.
2a	place familiar objects in chronological order.	putting a series of family photographs brought from home in the correct order; putting several historical objects used at school in the correct order; using a selection of pictures of various objects to put them in the order in which they were invented.
3a	describe changes over a period of time.	describing the changes which have happened and are shown in the pictures in 2a.
1b	give reasons for their own actions.	explaining why they have carried out any simple everyday action.
2b	suggest reasons why people in the past acted as they did.	suggesting why a person in the story used for 1a acted as they did.
3b	give a reason for an historical event or development.	using pictures of life in the past and giving reasons why things changed; using pictures with simple captions and circling one reason for the event or development shown.

2c	identify differences between past and present times.	telling the differences they have noticed in the pictures in 2a with regard to various objects; saying what is different from today in a picture about the past; circling on a photocopy of a picture from the past the things that are different.
3c	identify differences between times in the past.	identifying by circling or grouping into sets transport 100 and 400 years ago; discussing differences between clothes worn 100 and 400 years ago.

AT2 – interpretations of history The development of the ability to understand interpretations of history.

Level	Statements of attainment (Order, page 7)	Classroom activities
1	understand that stories may be about real people or fictional characters.	shown pictures of a fictional and of a real person, pointing to the one who really lived; drawing someone from a fairy story and someone who really lived; circling pictures of those characters who only appeared in fairy stories.
2	show an awareness that different stories about the past can give different versions of what happened.	discussing the different accounts of their own childhood given by different people.
3	distinguish between a fact and a point of view.	choosing which statement was 'what someone thought' from statements like 'Queen Victoria was a kind queen' and 'Queen Victoria lived a hundred years ago'.

AT3 – the use of historical sources The development of pupils' ability to acquire evidence from historical sources, and form judgements about their reliability and value.

Level	Statements of attainment (Order, page 9)	Classroom activities
1	communicate information acquired from an historical source.	discussing what they see in old photographs, or historical objects such as coins, or what they saw on a visit to a castle.
2	recognise that historical sources can stimulate and help answer questions about the past.	saying how the sources in 1 above help us to find out how people used to live; saying what they found out from them.
3	make deductions from historical sources.	saying what we can work out from sources like those in 1 above beyond what we can actually see in them.

Teaching and assessing at Key Stage 2

It was suggested above (page 9) that though the National Curriculum may make it more difficult to include history within thematic topics, these difficulties could be overcome, except perhaps with some of the core units. The topic webs in Figures 16 and 17 provide examples of a 'history-led' topic on 'Ancient Egypt' and a topic on 'Houses' where the history is only one of the subject areas emerging from the topic. Then follows a detailed account of lessons in Suffolk schools on a combined topic in which work on the core unit on the Anglo-Saxons is linked with work in English and technology, with detailed discussion of how children's work was assessed against attainment targets in all three subjects. Finally (pages 58 – 61) we include an exercise designed as part of a supplementary study unit on 'Land Transport'. This suggests work on sources on turnpike roads aimed at each of levels 1 to 7 of AT3 and discusses assessment at each of those levels.

Name _____ D. o. b _____

History in Key Stage 1

AT1 Knowledge and understanding	date	date	date	date	date
1a sequence events of historical story					
1b reasons for own actions					
2a objects in chronological order					
2b reasons for people's own actions					
2c differences between past and present					
3a describe changes over a period of time					
3b give a reason for an historical event or development					
3c identify differences between periods in the past					
AT2 Interpretations	date	date	date	date	date
1 difference between fictional and historical characters					
2 aware of more than one version of the past					
3 distinguish between a fact and a point of view					
AT3 Historical sources	date	date	date	date	date
1 communicate information					
2 can help answer questions about the past					
3 make deductions from historical sources					

Figure 15   *Assessment record sheet, Key Stage 1.*

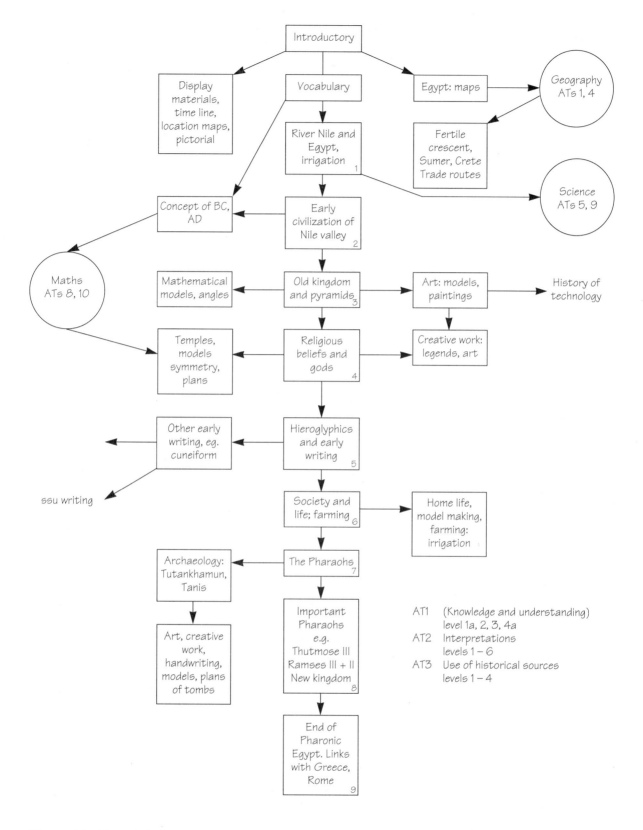

Figure 16 *History-led topic web: 'Ancient Egypt'.*

GEOGRAPHY

AT1: Geographical skills – mapwork

AT2 Local, UK, world – houses and resources

AT4: Human geography: patterns of population, settlement and economic activities

AT5: Environmental geography: use of the environment, past and present

SCIENCE

Electricity and magnetism (AT11, level 5):

1 Electricity as a source of power for domestic (TV, washers, etc.), social (signs, signals, etc.) industrial (machinery) use

2 How electricity works:
   (i) simple circuits
   (ii) conductivity
   (iii) control and safe use of electricity

3 magnets: their types, properties and uses

ART

Buildings:
– to promote awareness of surroundings
– use of colour
        lines
        tone
        shade

Park areas:
– compare differences and build on awareness

Building materials:
– texture
– develop individual collage of local area

Various media used throughout – pencil, crayon, charcoal, pen and ink

HISTORY

Study unit (supplementary A) Houses and places of worship. Development from Saxons to present day ('snapshot' approach)

Scheme of work will include:
(i) individual study/research on development of buildings/ architecture through the ages; (emphasis on chronology – AT1 (a))
(ii) fieldwork study of local buildings – AT3 (link with RE – churches, etc)

HOUSES AND THEIR HISTORY

MATHEMATICS

Maths work will follow SMP scheme and will be linked to the topic where appropriate

LANGUAGE

Language work will be linked to the topic where appropriate:

– use of information/ reference books
– writing for a range of purposes
– spelling relevant to the topic
– handwriting in accounts
– correct use of grammar

RE

Buildings and way of life in Palestine at time of Jesus; religious buildings of different faiths

Figure 17 *History-emerging topic web: 'Houses and their History'.*

A combined topic – history + English + technology

Aims and objectives   Core study unit 1 offers the opportunity for pupils to be taught about Anglo-Saxon invasions and settlements and specifically the legacy of settlement. This includes place names and language, myths and legends, styles of art and architecture.

The work which is described below sought to meet this section of the programme of study and was linked to work in English and technology in Key Stage 2. It involved the use of the historical source 'Beowulf' and a site visit to the reconstructed Anglo-Saxon village at West Stow in Suffolk. Assessment centred on the following attainment targets:

History AT3 – 'the use of historical sources', levels 2 – 5.

English AT3 – 'writing: a growing ability to construct and convey meaning in written language, matching style to audience and purpose'.

Technology AT1 – 'identifying needs and opportunities'.
          AT2 – 'generating a design'.
          AT3 – 'planning and making'.
          AT4 – 'evaluating'.

The introductory lesson   The lesson was taught in stages to a class of 8–9-year-olds and began with the class listening to Hugh Lupton's recorded version of 'Beowulf'. The teacher followed the listening by building an 'enabling vocabulary' with the class. The following list, which is not exhaustive, serves as an example:

hero	lord	golden	timber
sword	swamp	heat	metal
thatch	monster	bolts	axe
rafters	countryside	dagger	scales
weapons	armour	broad	straw
shield	brink	battle	bow
guard	candles	storyteller	arrow
hall	crowded	village	long ago
Denmark	farming	fields	crops

The first task   The class then listened to the tape for a second time with the task of writing down the information they learn from the source. Pupils were allowed to stop the tape wherever they wished and were asked to write down what they learnt about:

BUILDINGS	WEAPONS	AMUSEMENTS
CLOTHES	FOOD	JOBS

They were asked to specify both the information and the point in the story where they heard it. To differentiate pupil responses it was anticipated that a pupil reaching level 2 would identify four or more variables in each category. The samples of pupils' work shown here (samples 1 and 2) are differentiated between levels 1 and 2 in Figure 18.

The second task   After combing the source, pupils were then asked to retell in writing the story of 'Beowulf' or write a plausible alternative account which would have appealed to an Anglo-Saxon audience, and to illustrate their account. The class was allowed, if necessary, to listen

The great hall   Ian Newsor.
The Timbers.   Tnathed roof, Dim
Bolts. Straw roof. at the begining and
when grendaie came.
                    Weapons
Spears, Axes. Swords. daggers, hands.
Sticks. Sheilds. Armmour, boots.
metal plates.   helmets, When grendal
came for the second time,

Pupil sample 1

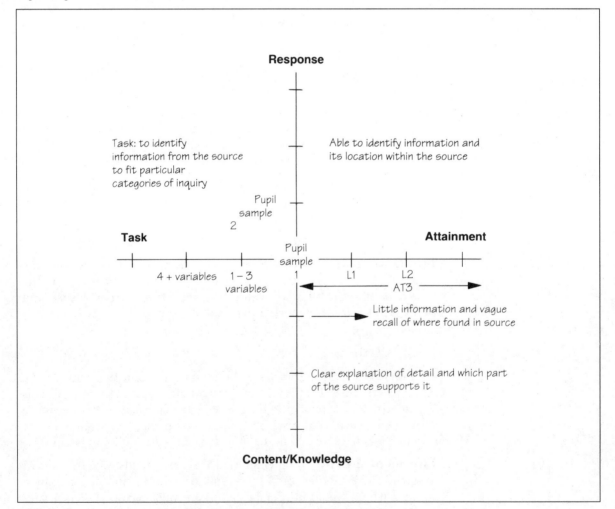

Figure 18   *Assessment and recording framework for pupil samples 1 and 2*

Anglo-Saxon's times - Beowolf

The Great Hall - They had straw thatch - when they said "The sun
                  beat down on it's golden thatch.
                  Timbers - Beginning
                  Rafters - Beginning
                  Candles - Begining
                  Dark - Beginning
                  Cold - When storyteller comes
                  Bolts - When Grendal come in
                  Small doors - When Grendal leaves
                  Timber Frames - Beginning
                  Crowded - When storyteller comes
Weapons - Spears - When Grendal comes in.
          daggers - When Grendal comes in.
          swords - When Grendal comes in.
          Bow and and arrow - when Grendal enters
          Shield - at the table, before the battle.
Food - Meat - At the table, before Beowolf passed over his weapon
       Bread - at the table, before the battle
       Drink - At the table, before the battle
       wine - At the table, before the battle
       Chicken - At the table, before the battle
       Fish - At the table, before the battle
Clothes -
        Rags - When Storyteller enters
        Armor - When Beowolf fights Grendal
        Animal skins - When Storyteller comes
        Chain vest - When Beowolf fights Grendal

Pupil sample 2

again to the tape. Before writing, the teacher led a discussion on the sorts of ideas the Anglo-Saxons would have expected in the plot, e.g. heroism, good v. evil, detailed description, etc. This discussion was, of course, in concrete terms rather than abstractions. For example:

'What sort of man was Beowulf?'
'How did the storyteller set the scene?'
'Why did Grendel deserve to be beaten?'

The written accounts from pupils, accompanied by drawings, were evaluated for language skills within the English AT3.

The history AT 3, level 3, was assessed according to how clearly the pupils deduced from the source what the great hall might have looked like and Grendel might have looked like. For example, pupil drawings of the 'monster' often resembled dinosaurs and an interesting class discussion focused on the fact that the Anglo-Saxon idea of a monster would probably have been quite different since dinosaur bones and reconstructions were unknown. Only one pupil (sample 3) drew a convincing Grendel, which resembled a grotesque human.

Samples 4 and 5 were marked, using Figure 19. Both pupil samples were judged to be operating at AT3, level 3.

Pupil sample 3

Lots of brave men came to fight the monster but none succeed. One day a brave man called Ethelred came to the kings great hall a said he had came to kill the monster. The king said you must be hungry after your long journey let us have a feast. They had roast oxen, roast mutton basted with honey, gravy, salmon spattered with butter and strong wine to drink. Then they went to sleep near the great fire. When they were sound asleep, The monster came out at night and broke the doors of peoples huts down, chopped their heads off with his arm, he bit he munched he spat and ate the peoples bodies up. Then he took their heads and buried them in the ground. The next day they realized that the terrible monster had came again in the night. There was fear and trembling every where. So Ethelred said I'll go and fight the monster now. You can borrow my white horse said the king.

Ethelred got his armour on. The weapons he carried were a shield, spears and a sword. Then he got on the ... white horse a rode off though the dark forest. Soon it was getting dark and misty the blackened trees looked as though they were alive, the mist was clinging to him. Rebecca
Slade

Daniel Woolland

Pupil sample 5

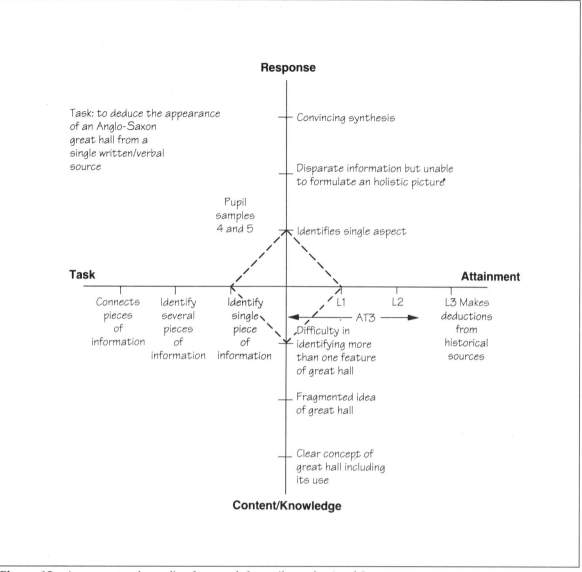

Figure 19 *Assessment and recording framework for pupil samples 4 and 5.*

The third task and site visit The teacher then brought together the pupil responses in a class discussion of Anglo-Saxon architecture. From the taped version of 'Beowulf' pupils were reminded that Anglo-Saxon buildings involved timber, rafters, thatch, doors with metal bolts, fire hearth, feasting tables, etc. The teacher then told the class that at the nearby Suffolk Anglo-Saxon village of West Stow the remains of buildings had been found. The remains consisted of no more than pits, post-holes and wooden fragments.

For the class the dig was simulated with sand trays (lids of cardboard boxes) arranged to simulate a pit and post-holes. Dowel rods, lollipop sticks and straw bundles simulated the fragments found. The pupils were then asked to construct the great hall as they would have expected it to look. This task formed part of a lesson which was planned to enable a visit to West Stow aimed to fulfil the design technology attainment targets as follows:

Design technology AT1 – identifying needs and opportunities The problem: evidence has been found of Anglo-Saxon buildings, i.e. pits, post-holes. These tell us about the foundations, but do not show what the buildings looked like at ground level or above. What sort of structures can be built using this evidence? NB Additional evidence – carbonised wooden planks, clay hearth pads.

Design technology AT2 – generating a design Use drawings, etc. to develop design proposals.

Design technology AT3 – planning and making Make a model of a structure using sand tray, wooden sticks and appropriate means of construction.

Design technology AT4 – evaluating Visit West Stow Anglo-Saxon village to see how evidence has been interpreted, the materials used, methods of construction used.

The site visit involves another exercise which enables answers to such questions as:

'Why were there pits?'

'What were the holes for?'

'How could timbers, rafters and thatch have looked when constructed?'

'How did they heat the building?'

The final task When asked to write about the visit and what they had found out, pupils began to meet the requirements of history AT3, level 5: to comment on the usefulness of an historical source by reference to its content. Pupils were asked to write a structured account from three prompts:

1 According to the Beowulf story I expected the great hall to look like this:

2 When we tried to make our model we thought . . .

3 At West Stow we discovered new things . . .

The pupil samples 6 and 7 are assessed in Figure 20.

How we put Beowulf together with our visit to West Stow Saxon village.

According to the Beowulf story I expected the Great Hall to look like this. I thought it would have a thatched roof made out of straw, wooden planks for a wall, and a big fire.

When we tried to make our model we thought the holes and the pit were for putting posts in and for storing food.

We built our hall like this, first we made a frame out of nine pieces of wood, then Daniel wove together some wood for the walls with elastic bands, then we made bundles of straw for the thatched roof. At West Stow we discovered new things and things we hadn't thought of before about how they built the hall. We measured the Great Hall it was 8 metres long, 4½ metres high and 3 metres wide. We found out how they made planks, they chopped down trees and got a wooden peg and split the tree into planks. Wooden pegs hold the planks together.

Pupil sample 6

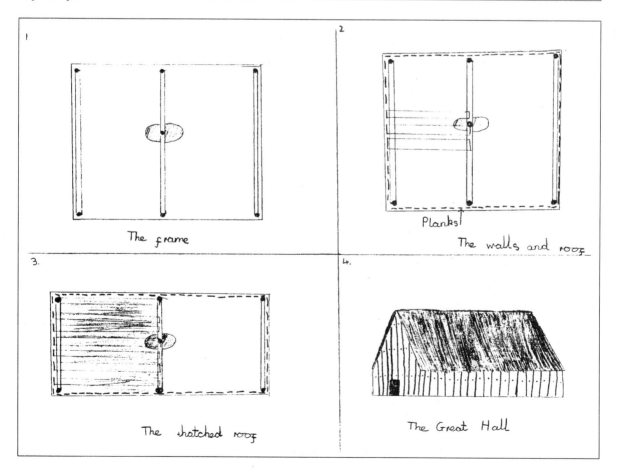

1.
The frame

2.
Planks
The walls and roof

3.
The thatched roof

4.
The Great Hall

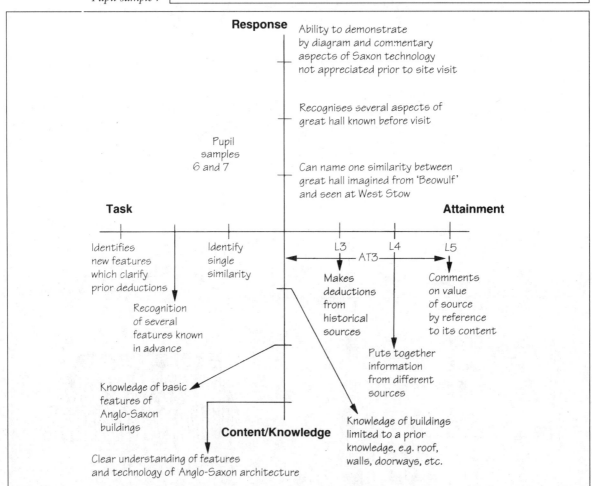

How we put Beowulf together with our visit to West Stow village.

According to the Beowulf story I expected the Great Hall to look like this. I thought the Great Hall would have a thatched roof made out of straw and wooden planks for walls.

When we tried to make our model we thought the holes and the pit were for putting posts in and the pit was for storing food in. We built our hall like this. First we made a frame out of nine pieces of wood then Daiel wove together some pieces of wood for the walls with rubber bands. Then we made bundles of straw for the thatched roof.

At West Stow we discovered new things and things we hadn't thought of before about how they built the hall. They used wooden pegs to hold the planks of wood for the walls and they had a hole in the roof so the smoke could get out.

Pupil sample 7

Response

Ability to demonstrate by diagram and commentary aspects of Saxon technology not appreciated prior to site visit

Recognises several aspects of great hall known before visit

Can name one similarity between great hall imagined from 'Beowulf' and seen at West Stow

Pupil samples 6 and 7

Task

Identifies new features which clarify prior deductions

Identify single similarity

Recognition of several features known in advance

Knowledge of basic features of Anglo-Saxon buildings

Clear understanding of features and technology of Anglo-Saxon architecture

Content/Knowledge

Attainment

L3 —— AT3 —— L4 —— L5

Makes deductions from historical sources

Puts together information from different sources

Comments on value of source by reference to its content

Knowledge of buildings limited to a prior knowledge, e.g. roof, walls, doorways, etc.

Figure 20 *Assessment and recording framework for pupil samples 6 and 7.*

Relating classroom activities to attainment targets and statements of attainment – an exercise on Turnpike Roads

The following exercise, using material on turnpike roads, was prepared for use with groups of teachers looking at the relationship between classroom activities and the assessment framework for history in the National Curriculum. It uses source material and ideas for questions which might form part of a local history unit on transport or of the Key Stage 2 supplementary unit 'Land Transport' (Order, page 31). AT3 is the main focus, though teachers may well be able to identify other attainment targets which could be approached through this material. The important factors are that the classroom activities are linked to progressive levels within AT3, and that they encompass a range of levels. Individual schools may wish to concentrate on a narrower range of levels. This exercise enables schools to consider framing a unit for a wide or a narrow ability range.

Figure 21 *Turnpike exercise, source A.*

Level 1 Communicate information acquired from an historical source. (For example, can talk about what can be seen in an old picture.)

Source A (Figure 21) Contemporary drawing of railway station scene, 1846. Pupils are simply invited to talk about the picture. Responses might include:

1 There is a train pulling several carriages.

2 There are two men on horseback.

3 Most people by the station are on foot.

Comments The statement of attainment is satisfied by a descriptive response leading in any direction. Only those responses which might arise regarding travel have been noted. Picture selection is clearly important; young children may not recognise the train in this picture.

Figure 22 *Turnpike exercise, Source B.*

Level 2 Recognise that historical sources can stimulate and help to answer questions about the past.

Sources A (page 55) and B (Figure 22), an 1845 stagecoach A question is required at this stage, presumably framed by the teacher rather than by the pupils. One possibility is: 'How can we find out about how people travelled before they had cars and buses?' Responses might include:

1 Use old pictures.

2 Ask old people.

Comments This requirement is more specific than that made for level 1; pupils' attention is directed to specific issues rather than being open-ended. However, their responses are still purely descriptive or factual.

Level 3 Make deductions from historical sources.

Source B (above) alone One approach here is to take a specific question again, but this time one which will enable them to infer (i.e. deduce) rather than merely to observe what is quite evident. The question might be: 'What was it like to travel by stagecoach?' In response, pupils might infer:

1 It could be uncomfortable to travel by stagecoach if you were an outside passenger, because it might be cold or raining.

2 It might be dangerous to travel outside, because you could fall down when getting off.

3 Stagecoaches would not travel very fast because they were pulled by horses.

Comments It has been assumed that pupils will be required to explain the inferences they have drawn. Questions could be posed to lead to a response, asking the pupils to reason out why this response is made. For instance, they might be asked: 'What clues are there to show you that coach travel could be uncomfortable or even dangerous?' (Teachers will think of more informal versions of this style.) Are there other inferential responses which pupils might make?

Level 4 Put together information drawn from different historical sources.

Sources B (above) and the following sources

Source C

> 'One had to go, patterns and all, outside a coach piled so high with luggage there was barely room to place your bottom, for 12 to 16 hours in cold, rain or snow and generally through the night.'

Letter from Evan Smith to William Sissons, 1850. The former was a partner in a Sheffield firm selling silver-plated articles. He carried his samples, or patterns, with him. They included teapots, candlesticks and trays.

Source D

> 'I know not in the whole range of language terms sufficiently expressive to describe this infernal road. Let me seriously caution all travellers . . . to avoid it as they would the devil. For a thousand to one, they will break their necks or limbs by over-throwing or breaking down. They will here meet with ruts which I actually measured four feet deep and floating with mud only from a wet summer. What must it therefore be in winter?'

Arthur Young, 'Tour through the North of England', 1771. He wrote of the road between Wigan and Preston in Lancashire.

Source E

> 'It was another affair altogether, a dark ride on top of the Tally-ho, I can tell you, in a tight Petersham coat and your feet dangling six inches from the floor. Then you knew what cold was, and what it was to be without legs, for not a bit of feeling you had in them after the first half hour.'

Source F

> (When the coach stopped at an inn, the guard told Tom to jump down, but this was easier said than done.)
> 'Tom finds a difficulty in jumping or indeed in finding the top of the wheel with his feet, which may be in the next world for all he feels; so the guard picks him off the coach top and sets him on his legs.'. . .

Thomas Hughes, 'Tom Brown's Schooldays', 1857. Tom took the Tally-ho coach to go from London to Rugby.

Sea Bathing.

The Public are respectfully informed that an OMNIBUS called

THE SAFETY

Will commence Running to the SIMPSON'S HOTEL,

BLACKPOOL,

On Wednesday, the 21st May, 1845,

From the HOLE IN THE WALL INN, in COLNE,

And from the OLD RED LION INN, BURNLEY,

Through Blackburn, Preston, and Lytham to Blackpool Three Times a Week, viz.—

On Wednesdays and Fridays from Colne, starting at Six o'clock in the Morning, and leaving Burnley at Seven o'clock, and reaching Blackpool at Two o'clock in the Afternoon, and on Monday Mornings from Burnley at Seven o'clock.

The above Omnibus will leave Blackpool returning to the above places every Tuesday, Thursday, and Saturday, at Ten o'clock in the Forenoon.

N. B. Arrangements will be made so that Passengers will be able to proceed through to Blackpool, without stopping except for change of Horses.

PERFORMED BY THE PUBLIC'S MOST OBEDIENT SERVANTS,

STUTTARD, ALLEN, & Co.

H. EARNSHAW, PRINTER, COLNE.

Figure 23 *Turnpike exercise, Source G*

Questions for pupils might include: 'How do these extracts help to show that stagecoach travel could be: (a) uncomfortable, (b) dangerous?'

Comments The questions seek to help pupils confirm hypotheses reached by looking at the stagecoach illustration and to use several sources to put an answer together. They might note, for example, the issue of poor road conditions adding to the danger of road travel. The teacher is still framing the scope of the enquiry.

Level 5 Comment on the usefulness of an historical source by reference to its content, as evidence for a particular enquiry.

Source G Stagecoach poster, 1845. Possible questions might include, 'Does the poster help you to find out about: (a) the route the coach took, (b) the time the journey took, (c) why the journey took as long as it did, (d) why people might travel on stagecoaches?'

Comments It is at this level that evaluation starts, rather than simply information gathering and using. The way the questions are phrased here may help pupils too much. Another approach would be just to ask them what the poster tells them about stagecoach travel. The first two questions above seek simple factual responses and the others deductions.

Level 6 Compare the usefulness of different historical sources for a particular enquiry.

Sources H, I and J *(Figures 24, 25 and 26)* The theme now extends from travelling by stage coach to toll roads. Pupils might be given the following text to start with:

'To make roads safer and easier for travellers, improvements were made. Money to do this was raised by charging travellers when they used a road. The payment they made was called a toll.

'Study the three sources. Write down what each of them tells you about how the toll system worked. Then say which of the sources was most useful in helping you to find this out. Clues are given to help you.

Figure 24 *Turnpike exercise, Source H: a toll bar on the Preston–Blackburn road (based on an old photograph).*

Figure 25 Turnpike exercise, Source I: from Yates's 1786 map of Lancashire.

Figure 26 Turnpike exercise, Source J: from the 1797 Act setting up the Blackburn–Bolton turnpike.

For every Score of Oxen or Neat Cattle, the Sum of Ten-pence; and so in Proportion for a greater or less Number :

For every Score of Calves, Sheep, Lambs, or Swine, the Sum of ̄ive-pence; and so in Proportion for a greater or less Number :

For every Coach, Chariot, Landau, Berlin, Chaise, Calash, Chair, ιravan, Hearse, Litter, or other such Carriage, drawn by Six or more orses, or other Beasts of Draught, the Sum of One Shilling ; and ιwn by Four Horses, or other Beasts of Draught, the Sum of Eight-nce ; and drawn by Two Horses, or other Beasts of Draught, the Sum Sixpence :

Source H: Think about what has been placed across the road and why. Also, think about who might have lived in the house.

Source I: Find the toll bar (TB) and think why it was placed there rather than nearer to Blackburn or further away. Remember, you would want to collect as much toll as possible.

Source J: Try to work out the basis on which toll charges were made. For instance, why was the toll higher for coaches drawn by six or four horses rather than by two? Think how road surfaces became worn.

Comments The difference between this and the level 4 exercise above is that the latter aimed at a specific problem or problems, presumably identified by the teacher, whereas this exercise asks pupils to work out a general conclusion about 'how the system worked', using more than one source, and to make decisions about the relative utility of sources.

Level 7   Make judgements about the reliability and value of historical sources by reference to the circumstances in which they were produced.

Sources   All could be used to develop this skill, but the poster (Source G) and travellers' accounts (Sources C and D) are particularly useful. The sort of issues pupils can be asked to address are:

Source G: 'The sea bathing poster is advertising a coach service. Can you think why the information it gives might not always have been true? (Clue: think why it might not always have been possible to keep to the timetable.)

'What impression does the poster give you about what it was like to travel by stagecoach? In what ways might it not give a true impression? How can this be explained?'

Travellers' accounts: What mood would Arthur Young have been in when he wrote his account? How might this have affected the description he gave of the road?

'Do you think these travellers give a balanced account of what it was like to travel by stagecoach? Explain your answer. (Clues: think about how many accounts you have here and about what the travellers did not write.)'

Comments   At this level, pupils seem to be moving from activities concerned with interpreting evidence to those associated with assessing its reliability.

Further suggestions   One theme that emerges in this topic is that of the speed at which stagecoaches travelled. Pupils could start with the stagecoach poster and, using a suitable map, trace the route and calculate the distance. Using the time data from the poster, they can then work out the average speed of the coach.

From the poster, they can find at least two reasons why stagecoaches would have been relatively slow. You might like to consider:

   1 Which other sources they would use to shed further light on this issue.

   2 What each of these sources would tell them.

   3 The level(s) at which such an activity would take place.

Teaching and assessing at Key Stage 3

To help to translate the rhetoric of the history National Curriculum into the hard currency of classroom practice we first take one core study unit – 'Medieval Realms c. 1066 to c. 1500' – and show how the themes listed could be turned into a series of lessons for year 7 pupils covering the content and developing the three attainment targets. That is followed by suggestions from two Lancashire schools, the first (page 70) for teaching AT1 within the core unit on 'The Roman Empire' and the second, an exercise (pages 69–75) aimed at levels 3–6 of AT2 in 'The Making of the UK'.

'Medieval Realms'

We are assuming a thirteen-week term for the unit with a double period (two × thirty-five minutes) and half-an-hour's homework every week. The Order (page 39) lists four themes with broad exemplars indicating areas from which content should be chosen. It is not necessary to stick rigidly to the order in which the exemplary topics are listed. You might, for example, think it better to deal with the 'Peasants' Revolt' after the Black Death and under the theme 'Medieval Society' rather than as part of the theme 'The Development of the English Monarchy'. For each theme, identify the topics you want to cover. Then for each topic, decide on the essential focus of your teaching and the attainment target or targets for which you will be aiming. Try wherever possible to use the particular, the concrete or the individual to illustrate the broader principle; for example, you might choose to focus on Joan of Arc, her part in the Hundred Years War and her trial by the church to exemplify the theme of 'Britain and the Wider World'. Then try to decide the amount of time you would wish to spend on each topic or cluster of topics. You might come up with a chart which looks something like Figure 27.

One useful way to start the unit would be to make a survey of topics to be covered, a timeline of the principal events and a family tree of the monarchs. To avoid making this a didactic, note-taking and copying lesson, the emphasis could be as follows. Introduce the unit dramatically; you might, for example, get the class to close their eyes while you set the scene of England in the year 1066, just before and after the Norman Conquest. Or you might get the class to sort out a random list of 'facts' about England in 1066 and in 1500 under the correct dates and under the headings of 'political', 'social', 'economic' and 'cultural'. The list could include such facts as 'no parliament', 'parliaments with an elected House of Commons help monarch to govern', 'country largely ruled by powerful barons', 'country united under strong central monarchy', 'Wales independent', 'Wales ruled by English king', 'French and Latin official languages', 'English official language', 'England trading with Europe alone', 'English traders beginning to reach beyond Europe for products and markets'. The main topics to be covered could then be given on a duplicated sheet and pupils could be asked to consider the two main questions they might wish to ask of each topic. They could then make a timeline from a list of events given on the board and construct a family tree from a written paragraph detailing the kings and queens of England during the period.

Themes/topics	Focus	Methods/materials	Time
Introduction	Period and topics to be covered: change and continuity (AT1)	Comparison of England 1066 with England 1500	1 week
The development of the English monarchy			
a) Norman Conquest	The Battle of Hastings: Causation (AT1)	– Simplified family tree of Edward the Confessor – Pictures of Bayeux Tapestry	1 week
b) Magna Carta	Magna Carta – the text Interpretations (AT2)	Historical controversies over the Charter: a comparison of secondary sources	1 week
c) Origins of Parliament	Parliament today – in 1500 – in C13th Change and continuity Sources (AT1, AT3)	Comparison and interpretation of: – contemporary photographs – picture of C15th parliament – description of 'model' parliament 1265	1 week
d) Relations between England, Ireland, Scotland and Wales	UK today – how united? 'UK' in 1066 'UK' in 1500 Change and continuity Interpretations (AT1, AT2)	– Comparison of maps Secondary accounts from Welsh or Scottish texts focusing on – e.g. Bannock Burn 1314	1 week
Medieval Society a) Feudalism Structure of medieval society	Castles: law and order Sources (AT3)	Site work if possible: otherwise working with pictures and diagrams	1 week
b) Beliefs and influence of the Church	Focus mainly on either parish church or Cathedral or Monastery	Site work if possible: otherwise working with pictures and diagrams	1 week
c) How material needs were met	Domesday sources, Barter: the economy Overseas trade Cause/consequence Interpretations Use of sources (AT1, AT2, AT3)	Domesday entry for particular town Role play game: Barter in the village Map work Overseas trade	2 weeks
d) Health and disease	Black Death Peasants' Revolt Cause and consequence (AT1, AT3)	Document evidence Effects of the Black Death; its connection with the Peasants' Revolt	2 weeks
Britain and the wider world	The hundred years war – Joan of Arc Interpretations (AT2)	The myth and the reality: how far was Joan the 'Saviour of France'?	1 week
The legacy of medieval culture	The English language	Chaucer's Canterbury Tales as a document – comparing original text with translation HW: retrospect: what else of the medieval world remains today?	1 week

Figure 27 *Core study unit chart of themes and topics, Key Stage 3.*

Example approach   Here is an example of one approach you might adopt when teaching one of the eleven topics or topic clusters listed in Figure 27. Topic (c) under the theme heading of 'Medieval Society' ('How material needs were met') focuses on the Domesday survey, the medieval economy and overseas trade. We have allowed two double periods plus two half-hour homeworks. The lesson could start by reminding the pupils of the conquest in 1066 and emphasising that it was not until the 1070s that the whole of England was firmly under Norman control. What might a foreign king then want to do? This could lead in to the circumstances which gave rise to the survey. It was compiled twenty years after the invasion of 1066. In the *Anglo-Saxon Chronicle* we are told that in 1085:

> 'at Gloucester at midwinter . . . the king had deep speech with his counsellors . . . and sent men all over England to each shire . . . to find out . . . what or how much each landowner held . . . in livestock, and what it was worth . . . The returns were to be brought to him.'

Pupils could consider how such a survey could be undertaken, given the conditions in 11th-century England. What sort of questions would the commissioners be told to ask? The results of this discussion (which could well be undertaken in small groups with a plenary report back) could then be compared with the brief given to commissioners in the region of Ely, Cambridgeshire.

Ely brief to the commissioners:

> 'The name of the place. Who held it before 1066 and now? How many hides (a land unit, reckoned as 120 acres)? How many ploughs, both those in lordship and the men's? How many free men? How much woodland, meadow and pasture? How many mills and fishponds? How much has been added or taken away? What the total value was and is? How much each freeman had or has? All threefold, before 1066, when King William gave it and now; and if more can be had than at present?'

The volume from Ely describes the procedure. The commissioners took evidence on oath 'from the sheriff; from all the barons and their Frenchmen; and from the whole Hundred, the priests, the reeves and six villagers from each village'. It also names four Frenchmen and four Englishmen from each Hundred who were sworn to verify the detail.

Worthwhile work can also be done by examining part of the document itself. A class of year 7 pupils at a Sussex school looked through the entries in Latin and in translation for two nearby towns, Chichester and Arundel (Figure 28).

They first worked in pairs to find out and jot down what they could from the Latin entries, half working on the Chichester entry and half on the Arundel. Then they pooled and discussed what they had found. The pairs then went on to look at the English translation, and to consider what they could learn from that. What did they think King William would do with the knowledge he had gathered? Once again the findings were pooled in a plenary session.

118 The Count holds MAYFIELD (?) himself. Godwin held it. Then and now for 4 hides. Land for 2 ploughs. They are there, with 4 villagers and 5 smallholders. In lordship 1 plough.
From woodland 30 pigs.
Value before 1066 £4; now 40s.
Of this land, William of Warenne holds 3 virgates of land and 1 mill.

23 a

LAND OF EARL ROGER
(Chichester and Arundel Rapes)

11

1 In the City of CHICHESTER before 1066 there were 100 sites less 2½ and 3 crofts. They paid 49s less 1d. This city is now in Earl Roger's hands. In the same dwelling-sites there are 60 more houses than there were before.
A mill at 5s.
They paid £15; £10 to the King, 100s to the Earl; value now £25; however they pay £35.
Humphrey Flambard has 1 site there at 10s.

2 ARUNDEL CASTLE before 1066 paid 40s from a mill; 20s for 3 banquets; and 20s for 1 entertainment. Now the Borough and the harbour and the ship customs between them pay £12; value, however, £13, of which St. Nicholas' has 24s.
A fishery at 5s; a mill which pays 10 measures of wheat and 10 measures of rough corn; 4 measures in addition. This is assessed at £14.
Robert son of Theobald has 2 sites at 2s; he has his tolls from strangers. Morin has customs dues there from 2 burgesses at 12d; Arnold 1 burgess at 12d; St. Martin's 1 burgess at 12d; Ralph 1 site at 12d; William 5 sites at 5s; Nigel 5 sites which do service.

23 a

Ipſe com̃ ten̄ 7 MÆSFUFELLE. Goduñ tenuit. T̃c 7 m̃ .p. ɪɪɪɪ. hid. Tra. ē. ɪɪ. car. 7 ibi ſunͭ cũ . ɪɪɪɪ. uillis . 7 . v . bord . In dñio . ē una caͬ.
De ſilua:́ .xxx. porc . T. R. E. uatͮ . ɪɪɪɪ . lib . m̃́. xͰ. ſolid̃.
D̃e hac tra . ten̄ Witͮs de Ŵareue . ɪɪɪɪ . uirg̃ tͬͰe . 7 uñ moliͭ.

23 a

.XI. ## TͦERRA COMITIS ROGERII.

In̄ CICESTRE Ciuitate . T . R . E . erant . c . hagæ . ɪɪ . 7 dim min.
7 . ɪɪɪ . croftæ . 7 reddeb . xLɪx . ſolid . uñ denar min.
Modo eſt ipſa ciuitas in manu comitis Rogerii . 7 ſunt in eiſdͤ maſuris . Lx . domͤ pluſq̃ã antea fuerant . 7 ibi uñ moliñ de . v . ſolid . Reddeb . xv . lib . Regi: x . lib . comiti: c . ſolꝭ
Modo uaͭ xxv . lib . 7 taͭñ redd . xxxv . lib.
Hunfrid̃ h̃t ibi . ɪ . hagã de . x . ſolid.

CͤASTRͦU HARUNDEL . T . R . E . reddeb de ꝓꝉã molino . xL . ſolid . 7 de . ɪɪɪͭ . conuiuis . xx . ſolid . 7 de uno paſſicio . xx . ſoͭ.
Modo int burgͤu 7 portũ aq̃ue 7 c̃ſuetudiñͤ nauiũ redd xɪɪ . lib . 7 taͭñ uaͭ . xɪɪɪ . liͮ . de his h̃ S̃ Nicolaus xxɪɪɪɪ.
ſolid̃ . Ibi una piſcaria de . v . ſolid . 7 uñ moliñ reddꝭS x . modia fruͭñti . 7 x . modia groſſæ annoͭæ . Inſuꝑ . ɪɪɪɪ . modia.
Hoc apꝓciaͭ̃ . ē . xɪɪɪɪ . lib.
Roͭbt fili Tetbaldi h̃t . ɪɪ . hagas de . ɪɪ . ſolid . 7 de hoͭibⱫ extneis h̃t ſuͭ theloneͭu.
Morin h̃t ibi c̃ſuetud de . ɪɪ . burgͤibⱫ . de . xɪɪ . denar.
Ernald̃ uñ burgͤe de . xɪɪ . den . S̃cs Martin . ɪ . burgͤe de . xɪɪ . den.
Radulf̃ unã hagã de . xɪɪ . den . Witͮs . v . hagas de . v . ſolid.
Nigellus . v . hagas q̃ue faciunt ſeruitiͭu.

Figure 28 Domesday Book entries for Chichester and Arundel.

In the third stage of the work the pupils as individuals tackled the following tasks.

1 Can these statements be supported with evidence from the documents?

(a) Chichester was a growing town.

(b) The citizens of Chichester were taxed too highly.

(c) There were different ways of paying tax.

(d) Towns were a good source of money for the king.

2 Why might towns want to run themselves rather than belong to a king or a lord?

The tasks are sharply focused on AT3 and they cover its first five statements of attainment:

1 Communicate information acquired from a historical source.

2 Recognise that historical sources can stimulate and help answer questions about the past.

3 Make deductions from historical sources.

4 Put together information drawn from different historical sources.

5 Comment on the usefulness of an historical source by reference to its content, as evidence for a particular enquiry.

Two examples of pupils' responses to the tasks are shown as samples 8 and 9. See if you can plot each on the four-dimensional assessment model discussed on page 22. You should consider the Task (what it is the pupil is required to do), the Response (the way in which each pupil copes with the task), the Attainment (the target and levels) and the Content/Knowledge (the kinds of historical information, conceptual understanding or skill each pupil is able to use).

A lesson such as this might be followed by work on the ideas of towns and trade and the ways in which coinage was gradually penetrating the old barter economy in medieval times. The role-play 'Barter' is an excellent way of addressing this issue.

'Barter' role-play   It is autumn 1270: pupils are given roles in the Yorkshire village of Appleton-le-Moors. There is a miller, a blacksmith, a carpenter, a cobbler, a priest (the rector); there are families of sheep farmers, weavers, livestock raisers and peasants farming their strips. All want to survive the winter; their produce or skills alone are not enough. How can they trade and bargain with their neighbours to gain the food, clothing, footwear and repair materials which will enable them to survive the winter? Tokens can be used to represent the goods or services which each has to offer. A certain amount of coinage is also in circulation. After the game has been played, the class can discuss the problems which a barter economy produced. Does barter have any advantages over money? Did any villagers become particularly unpopular in the village as bartering took place? Did the presence of money make things easier or more difficult? (Full details of the game

Domes Day Book.   Jenica Workwork.

1. You can learn that there is a spelling dyperece.
2. They have Roman Numerals for there numbers.
3. They do not have full senteces.
4. The have strange signs above there words.
5. They have capital letters halfway though there sentences.
6. I think Terra comitis Rogeri as well as means the land of Roger.
1. They are shillings   pence.
2. chichester was growing.
3. The city was in Earl Roger's hard.
4. They paid money to the King.
5. Hamphrey Flambard has quite a lot of money.

1. chichester was a growing town because more people went to live there, so they needed to build more houses.
2. No because they need the money to build houses and get food.
3. Yes there were because they could give animals to pay. They could give something from there shops. They could work for them. OR if they had a Job they could give something from there.
4. True because he could get people to work for him. Have a good food place and have very good crops. He could get a good % from there shops and get good money for taxes.
5. They could tell people about it. Lower the Tax rate. You can ask for food if you have no money.
6. Arundel don't have a lord. They don't have as many sites. They would not have to pay tax. They wouldn't have to pay the Earl or the king. They would be more free without being told what to do. They would not have to entertain for the king or be his cooks or things like that. They wouldn't be punished for steeling or killing people.

Pupil sample 8

<u>Pomesday Book</u>

1. They have different spelling.
2. They use Roman numerals.
3. They don't use full stops or punctuation.
4. They don't have proper sentances.
5. They use capital letters alot.
6. They have a squiggle above the person name.
7. They use capital letters for names like us.
   We learn from the English that:-
1. Before 1066 there were 100 sites.
2. They paid money to the king.
3. The city was in Earl Roger's hand.
4. They paid in pounds and shillings.
5. Rumphrey Flambard has 1 site there at 10 shillings.
6. In the same place there are 60 more houses than there were before.
7. They paid £15; £10 to the king.
8. They paid 100 shillings to the Earl.

1. Chichester was a growing town because it tells you how many
   sites there were and how its grown.
2. The citizens of Chichester were taxed to high because the king
   needed more money to build up the town.
3. The different ways of paying rent are with crops or animals
   or produce, land and servants and clothes.
4. Towns were a good source of money for the king because
   he could go round collecting the taxes.
5. The king could use the knowledge by finding out if the Earl
   is doing the right job and also if the residents are being
   taxed too high. And how much land there is.
6. The differences between Chichester and Arundal are Arundal
   has a harbour and more entertainment and Chichester seems
   more quiet and developed.
7. They have higher taxes in Chichester than in Arundal.
8. The towns might want to run themselves because
   they would'nt have to pay tolls or taxes and they would
   also have freedom and would not have to just stay in
   the town all the time they could sort of wonder
   around.

Pupil sample 9

can be found in *Involvement in History*, general editor David Birt; *The Middle Ages II* by Robin Acland and David Birt, Edward Arnold, 1979.)

The pupils could then go on to think about the ways in which the economy expanded and barter gave way increasingly to trade which was based on money and was often national or international. Towns grew up and developed both as staging posts and as centres of trade. A sheet could be given to pupils which briefly introduces this topic and directs them to a map of medieval trade routes (for example, the map on page 89 of the Collins *Past into Present* series, Book 1, 1988). Pupils could be asked to list the imports to England under the headings of 'luxury foods/drink', 'luxury goods', 'basic foods', 'basic goods'. 'What was virtually the only export from England? How important do you think this export was? Explain your answer. Why was there only one export? Can we tell anything about the standard of living in medieval England from this map? What other sources of evidence might you want to consult in order to find more evidence about the standard of living?'

'The Roman Empire' A plan for assessing AT1 at three stages of work on the Roman Empire core unit is shown in Figure 29.

'The Making of the UK' This piece of work is focused on attainment target 2, levels 3–6, and provides activities which enable pupils to demonstrate their understanding, related to the various statements of attainment. The task could be done either as a written assignment or as an orally discussed classroom activity. In both cases pupils' responses could be assessed and recorded. It could also be used wholly as a teaching activity – perhaps by going through the sources and discussing ideas of different views in class and then giving the questions to the pupils as a written homework exercise.

It is assumed that the pupils will have done some background work on the reasons for the opposition of some – especially the Highland – Scots to the Hanoverian English monarchs ruling Scotland, and so can approach the context of this task with some knowledge and understanding of the situation.

Level 3 Distinguish between a fact and a point of view.

The first three questions try to approach this, using a number of short written sources and two pictorial ones. The first three sources need to be read before attempting the first question.

Source A

'At Prestonpans, about twelve miles from Edinburgh, there was a fine battle. The King's troops were defeated, with the loss of 500 men. The confusion was so great that if Charles Edward had used his advantages at that time, and entered England, he would probably have achieved his aim – the throne. But with his usual silliness and weakness, he remained, wasting away his time in pretending to be King in Edinburgh.'

From a school history book written in the 19th century.

Context:

- 'The Roman Empire' is a core study unit (1) National Curriculum at Key Stage 3 history
- At Primet we are scheduled to teach a 'The Roman Empire' unit in March/April/May 1991 to year 7 (dependant upon teaching group). It seems sensible to trial various strategies before next year.
- Suggested approach is *one* possible pathway through ATs and levels. Whatever approach is eventually adopted, the 'assessment tasks' must become an integral part of classroom activity and they would *not* necessarily be the culmination of several weeks' work.
- Considered on aspect of 'The Roman Empire' unit
  - ways of life
  - family and society related to AT1 and levels 4, 5 and 6 (strand (c)). Differentiation is achieved by task, but it is recognised that differentiation by outcome, or indeed a combination of both, could be used on other occasions.
- Emphasis is on the application of 'discovered' knowledge, rather than the passive transmission of information from teacher to pupil.
- Hopefully paid attention to the needs of youngsters who have learning difficulties. Often they are disadvantaged, not by the complexity of the task, but by the complexity of the instructions they receive. Therefore eventual tasks will adhere to these guidelines:
  - clear, concise at an appropriate reading age;
  - short sentences which give instructions;
  - tasks to incorporate opportunities to 'describe', 'identify' and 'show' by other means *apart* from producing writing
  - opportunity for all youngsters to achieve at any level;
  - 'assignment tasks' to be kept as brief as possible, hereby allowing pupils some opportunity for their own contributions and initiatives;
  - full use made of special needs/support teams in providing range of materials.
- Lessons in between these would cover key elements outlined in the **POS** for Key Stage 3 relevant to the Roman Empire. In addition the three ATs would be taught interdependently and *not* as a series of lessons on AT1, AT2 and then AT3.

Lesson no. and topic	Pupil outcomes	Teaching/learning strategies	Cross – curricular			Assessment
			Skills	Themes	Dimensions	
6	Pupils should be able to: Describe different features of an historical situation (independent aspects of life in Roman society).	Using library/video/textbooks/database/own resources. Pupils collect, collate, arrange, label and display relevant pictures, maps and diagrams and written work all of which illustrate life in Roman society. *Activities* (any of which ought to lead to AT1 L4(c)): 1 Prepared illustrations, maps, with various options/statements. Series of cloze passages and directed questions. 2 Use of IT/word processing to organise and present researched information. 3 Tape recording to orally describe features. 4 Use of illustrations. Drawing, painting & model making. 5 Written work using titles/subheadings of their own and 'supplied' headings.	Information technology AT5, L4(a)	These can be incorporated throughout with the relevant statement to demonstrate exactly *when/where* it is being delivered		AT1, Level 4(c)
10	Describe how different features in an historical situation relate to each other (account of life in Rome or a province *linking* food, Empire, slaves, society and family, for example).	Based on a series of background lessons, pupils undertake one of the following activities: 1 Prepare and perform a documentary programme about people with different perspectives: Roman citizen vs. villager 2 Produce a jigsaw with diagrams, drawings and written information to show links between Roman society. 3 Spray diagram/poster for wall display showing links. 4 Specific task (essay).				AT1, Level 5(c)
13	Describe the ideas and attitudes of people in an historical situation (planning a new house, discussing possible treatment for an illness, religion and the gods, the arts, for example).	Pupils undertake any *one* of the following activities: A Situation *provided* to pupils. 1 Planning a new house 2 Religion and Gods *activity* – draw plan – conversation – perform – write – record 3 Family meal discussion – extended piece of B Pupils contrive their own situation writing				AT1, Level 6(c)

Figure 29   *Strategy for the teaching and assessment of one AT within a core study unit, Key Stage 3, year 7.*

Source B

'I intend to go shooting again, but not when it rains.'

A comment made by Prince Charles Edward while he was in France, just before he set off for Scotland.

Source C

'None but a mad fool would have fought that day.'

A comment made by Lord Lovat, one of Prince Charles Edward's supporters, about Charles's decision to fight at Culloden.

Question 1   What do Sources A, B and C tell us about Prince Charles Edward as *a person*?

Sources D–G need to be looked at before attempting questions 2 and 3.

Source D

'The Prince brought along with him four shirts, a cold cooked chicken, a bottle of brandy and a lump of sugar. All these (adding to them a bottle of whisky he bought from a landlord on the Island of Skye) he took along with him to the Island of Raasay.'

From a verbal statement made in 1748 by a man who lived on the Island of Raasay. Raasay is an island near Skye, and Prince Charles Edward hid there after the Battle of Culloden.

Source E (Figure 30)

Figure 30   *Source E: a drawing from a story in a children's annual published in 1954; the prince is the figure with his back to us; he has just been handed a gift of money from one of his loyal supporters*

Source F

> 'Burnt are our homes;
> Exile and death scatter the loyal men.
> Yet, ere the sword cool in the sheath,
> Charlie will come again.

> 'Speed, bonnie boat like a bird on the wing!
> "Onward!" the sailors cry.
> Carry the lad who is born to be king
> Over the sea to Skye.'

The last verse of the 'Skye Boat Song', a traditional Scottish folk song, written down in 1884.

Source G (Figure 31)

Figure 31 *Source G: two drawings of Prince Charles Edward, made at the time of the 1745 rebellion, when he was 25 years old.*

Question 2 Explain carefully which of these sources (D, E, F and G) best shows Bonnie Prince Charlie as a hero.

Question 3 Look again at Sources A–G. Choose ONE of these which you think gives the most realistic idea of what Prince Charles was like. Explain why you have chosen this source.

Levels 4 and 5 Show an understanding that deficiencies in evidence may lead to different interpretations of the past.

Recognise that interpretations of the past, including popular accounts, may differ from what is known to have happened.

For question 4 the pupils will need to look again at sources E and G and then to read a further short written source (Source H). For question 5, which tries to reinforce understanding of the ideas in this level and question 6, which takes them on to level 5, they will need to read two further short written sources (sources I and J).

Source H

'Prince Charles was hiding in the west of Scotland. His red beard was growing and his tartan was tattered.'

From a book written recently by a Scottish historian about Prince Charles Edward.

Question 4 Look again at the drawings of the prince in Sources E and G. Then read Source H. Why do you think they give different ideas about what the prince looked like?

Source I

'Although a reward of £30,000 was offered for his head, not even the poorest Scot who knew where to find him was mean enough to betray him. After numerous dangers he escaped to the continent and died in Rome in 1788.'

From a school history book written in the early 20th century. This is referring to the time after Culloden, when Prince Charles was in hiding

Source J

'One of the ideas passed down about Bonnie Prince Charlie is that no one in the Highlands could be found who would betray him. The truth of the story is that the government had spies among the clansmen who would most certainly have betrayed him if it had been possible.'

From a book published in 1961 about the Battle of Culloden.

Question 5 Read Sources I and J. Why do you think that Source I says that no one would betray the prince but Source J says that some would?

Question 6 Do you think that it is likely that some of the clansmen were government spies? Or do you think that Source I is right?

Level 6 Demonstrate how historical interpretations depend on the selection of sources.

This next stage could well be omitted unless some or all of the pupils were able to understand its significance. The activity involves them grouping the given sources in different ways to support different conclusions about Prince Charles Edward.

Question 7   Now look at all the sources which you have used for this task. As you have seen, they give various different ideas about Prince Charles. First of all make two columns, one headed 'Charles the hero' and the other headed 'Charles the failure'. Then list the sources under the different columns. Some may not fit in either column – that does not matter. Do you feel that you can come to a decision about what Prince Charles Edward was really like? If so, why? If not, why not?

Assessment   An assessment diagram for this exercise is shown in Figure 32:

T: This is divided into seven parts, and is related to the various ways Prince Charles Edward was portrayed at the time and later, and also to approaching an understanding of the reasons for different interpretations.

R: Relates to the ability:

- to recognise e.g. the difference between a fact and a point of view and the fact that accounts do differ; and

- to explain these differences in valid terms.

A: Shows the four levels covered by the questions.

C/K: Relates to the level of ability of the pupil to deal with the sources/questions unaided.

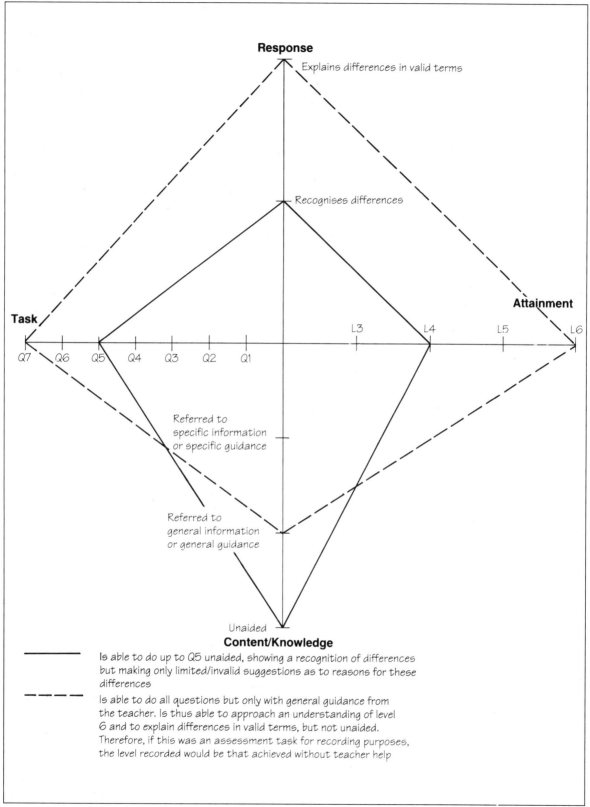

Response

Explains differences in valid terms

Recognises differences

Task

Q7 Q6 Q5 Q4 Q3 Q2 Q1

L3 L4 L5 L6

Attainment

Referred to
specific information
or specific guidance

Referred to
general information
or general guidance

Unaided

Content/Knowledge

———— Is able to do up to Q5 unaided, showing a recognition of differences
but making only limited/invalid suggestions as to reasons for these
differences

– – – – Is able to do all questions but only with general guidance from
the teacher. Is thus able to approach an understanding of level
6 and to explain differences in valid terms, but not unaided.
Therefore, if this was an assessment task for recording purposes,
the level recorded would be that achieved without teacher help

Figure 32 *Assessment and recording framework for 'Prince Charlie and the '45', Key Stage 3.*

4 LOCAL HISTORY IN THE NATIONAL CURRICULUM

Why teach local history?

'The student had prepared well for the pupils' first lesson on the Second World War. Assembled in front of them were a gas mask, ration book, ARP warden's tin hat, identity card, photograph of a young man in Home Guard uniform and a wartime recipe book. They all belonged to the same family. The pupils were allowed to touch, look, read and try on. The first half of the lesson was full of lively discussion. All was going well. Then disaster struck. Calling for silence, the student smiled: "Now, why was it that people had to live like this with gas masks at the ready, ration books and identity cards? Well, in 1933 a man called Adolf Hitler came to power in Germany . . ." We were then off into a routine trot up to 1939.'

(College of Education tutor, observing a school practice)

Local history is certainly far more than the illustrating of national or world history with some tasty local snippets. It should help to explain that which is national and global, not just embellish it. A study of how a family of out-workers lived and worked 170 years ago in the cottage up the road will provide far greater insights into the workings of the woollen industry and the problems involved in introducing mechanisation than any teaching of bland generalisations.

Here, too, lies academic credibility. The generalisations which too often form national history can only be created from an amalgam of local histories. This is particularly true of social and economic history. The greater the evidence which can be trawled up from the localities about, for example, the effects of enclosure upon landless labourers, the sooner will national generalisations be qualified or even changed. Small-scale limited studies by pupils can make a valuable contribution to the shifting national picture.

A study of local history involves using the pupils' locality as the area of historical enquiry. Pupils should never be taught local history as a received body of knowledge: the very best local history work is always of an investigative nature. This requires the utilisation of the whole historical process, involving both skills and understanding. Inevitably a variety of source material will be involved. Skills such as observation, comprehension, inference, evaluation and synthesis will be needed; these skills, however, cannot and must not be developed and used in isolation. They must be used to enable pupils to come to a greater understanding of the past. In achieving this, pupils will have been introduced to the idea of chronology; to an understanding of change and development, of similarity and difference, of cause and consequence and of motivation. They should, too, have been encouraged to compare their findings with the general national pattern and to draw suitable inferences which may, in turn, provide starting points for further local investigations within a school.

This sense of chronology, of change and continuity over time in a local context, can give a potentially rootless pupil a sense of belonging to the community in which he or she lives. Few children live in the community in which their parents were children, in which their aunts and uncles went to school and their grandparents married. The years since 1945 have seen an almost unprecedented destruction of old communities and the erection of new towns and estates in their place. Thousands of children will move house and change school more than once during the years of compulsory schooling. A study of local history can provide, for many such children, the security of understanding their new community, fostering a sense of ownership and belonging.

Above all, local history is an intrinsically interesting field of study for itself alone. It combines academic credibility with a rigorous application of skills and understanding which can be made acceptably appropriate for pupils of all ages, and it fosters that most basic of all historians' qualities – curiosity.

The raw materials of local history

Buildings and artefacts are a natural starting point for most pupils, particularly younger ones. Observing and recording what the barn, house, mill and shop look like will lead naturally to questions such as:

- Why was it built?

- Why was it built like that?

- Who built it?

- When?

- Who lived/worked there?

- What was it like to live/work there?

These questions can only be answered by consulting other source material. Plans, photographs, newspaper reports, census returns, wage books, household accounts, diaries and letters may all have something useful to say, provided they can be found. This does not mean that teachers embarking on a local history course must have done many hours of archival work beforehand. A single photograph can answer the question 'Has this building always been a garage?' and should lead to further investigations of social change at a local level.

The questions evoked by an object can develop in a similar way. Questions like:

- What does it look like?
- What is it made of?
- Has it been made by hand or machine?
- What was it used for?
- Does it do this job effectively?
- What is it worth?

will all lead to the need to explore further local source material.

Pictures and photographs are a stimulating resource for local history. They must never, however, be regarded as an easy alternative to a written source. Both paintings and photographs can be unreliable evidence of anything beyond their perpetrators' intent. It is too easy for pupils to fall into the trap of seeing paintings as untrue and photographs as true, or into the opposite trap of accepting all paintings and drawings as reliable and all photographs as 'fixed'. Having said that, an investigation of any picture, if carefully structured, is well within the compass of the whole ability range at all key stages. Questions can start with the surface features:

- What is she wearing?
- Is the dress posh or working class?
- Can you tell, from his clothes, that he is a working man?

From here it is a short and natural step to begin to ask the sorts of question which raise issues about the provenance and possible reliability:

- Why would this person want their photograph taken/portrait painted?
- Why would someone want to take a photograph of pit-brow girls?
- Why would they want their photograph taken?
- Is this photograph posed?
- Is this painting accurate?
- Why would an artist want to spend hours painting a distant view of industrial Bradford?

Photographs and paintings can spark off a discussion on dress, transport, housing conditions, sport, leisure activities and social class. Properly guided, this can lead to a fuller exploration of specific aspects of the life of a community. They can also be used to provide further evidence when testing tentative conclusions or hypotheses based on other sources.

Some schools begin to develop the idea of chronology by encouraging pupils to write their own family history. There are plenty of commercially available publications which encourage pupils to fill in their own family trees. This approach is a perfectly valid aspect of local history, and can encourage the handling and evaluation of all kinds of source material. It should, however, be treated with extreme care. Real distress can be caused to adopted children, children in care, children with family backgrounds and patterns of parenting which are not the standard ones of western Europe, and children from families with skeletons in cupboards. Some families quite simply want to keep private what they consider to be their own business. It may be that the most sensitive approach is via an imaginary family. One teacher made successful use of her own family, which had no skeletons but lots of evidence in its cupboards.

Oral history is a rich seam to mine. While taped interviews with people from all kinds of occupations and social class can usually be obtained from the local record office or local studies library, this can rarely compare with pupils gaining this kind of first-hand evidence for themselves. Pupils doing this need to be well versed in the use of a tape recorder, and should have prepared a questioning structure for the interview. 'What was it like when you were a girl?' is unlikely to yield as much of interest as a structured sequence of questions dealing with issues of smaller compass:

- What did you wear when you were my age?

- What sort of things did you eat for breakfast/dinner/tea?

- What games did you play?

- Where did you first go to work?

- What did you like best/least about going to work?

Pupils must be encouraged to listen to what is being said to them, and to ad-lib a follow-up question if the answer merits it. A response ending '. . . . but of course it was different after August' invites the interviewer to ask why it was different after August.

Oral evidence can then be fitted into the general local and national pattern. Pupils should be reminded of the vagaries of the human memory, although it would be unwise to suggest that memories of, say, the Blitz should be openly challenged in any way. The function of local history is not to start family or community feuds.

Radio and TV, films, pageants and local festivals are all rich and varied sources to quarry, particularly when the local community is involved in a pageant or festival. The origins of the event, whether it is well-dressing or a Wakes-Week walk, can be investigated using local sources. The main problem will come if the history being produced for mass consumption is over-romanticised or just plain wrong. A skilful teacher can nevertheless turn this to good effect by enabling pupils to evaluate the available evidence, and then by encouraging suggestions of reasons for the romantic presentation of the individual or event.

Availability and accessibility

Sources relating to a specific locality can be found in a bewildering variety of places. They will differ according to the policy of the local town, city or county and will also vary in respect of the particular type of source which is being sought. Record offices and central libraries will hold most of the material teachers will wish to use. Record offices are usually located in the administrative centre of the county. It must be remembered, however, that the main objective of record offices is to preserve the archive, not to act as a resource base for teachers. There may be problems in obtaining access to some material and almost certainly problems with borrowing or copying material for class use. Education officers or advisory teachers have sometimes been appointed to record offices and other archives and they can be invaluable. The primary job of libraries, on the other hand, is to educate. The main library in a town will almost certainly hold a range of material. Large libraries often have a local studies or local history department, and staff who will advise on the availability of specific material.

As a general rule, record offices hold manuscript material, and libraries hold printed records. Thus, newspapers, census returns and photographs are more likely to be housed in libraries; wills, inventories and land tax returns in a record office. However, this is not always the case. Some record offices collect printed material such as photographs and some libraries have archive material relating to a local workhouse or business. Diocesan archives may hold material relating to church activities; records such as baptism, marriage and burial registers have often been deposited in the county record office – but much still remains in the church vestry. National and international organisations such as the BBC and ICI have their own archives. Estate records and those of prominent local families might still be found on the estates if they have not been deposited in the local library or county record office. It is worth bearing in mind that the terms of the deposit may limit access and/or use. A local museum may hold source materials such as artefacts, posters, photographs and diaries. The Museum Education Service, in areas where it is adequately funded and flourishing, could hold collections of artefacts and other sources which may be directly relevant to the local theme being studied. Some investigations may depend upon archaeological evidence, and here contact with the local archaeological unit, many of which have education officers, will prove invaluable.

Careful planning is essential, no matter what type of local history investigation is being undertaken. The theme has to be selected, the likely source material identified – and the custodian of that material contacted. It is always sensible to write to the individual concerned, outlining the theme and the type of source material it is hoped to use, and asking for an appointment at a mutually convenient time to discuss the undertaking. Not only can advice then be given on the nature, condition and availability of source material, but hitherto unthought-of sources may well be suggested. This planning needs to be done well in advance and might involve co-operation with other schools in the area. Two large schools working simultaneously on, say, 'the workhouse' could create enormous problems. An ideal situation might involve a group of schools working with the local adviser/inspector, developing a theme in conjunction with local libraries/record offices, arranged in such a way that individual schools could work on the theme at different times of the school year. No matter how enthusiastic pupils are, they should never be encouraged to visit any archives unaccompanied, unannounced or unprepared. It is every librarian's nightmare to be faced with a day of unexpected visits from assorted children all saying 'I'm doing a project on the local canal. What have you got?'.

The quality of available source material is likely to be very variable and this will not necessarily have anything to do with age. Newspapers printed 1914–18 are, for example, very fragile because of the type of paper used during this time of national emergency. No record office or library allows the public to work with very fragile documents. Too much could be inadvertently destroyed. Given sufficient notice, staff will often provide photocopies instead but this can prove costly if multiple copies are involved. Some source material which is used frequently, such as local newspapers and census returns, is often available on microfilm.

It is important that careful thought is given to the way pupils will physically use source material. Would, for example, the whole class work on the same records, or would different groups of pupils work with different records? If the latter is the case, how could one ensure that all pupils had experience of all sources – or would this not matter? Indeed, would a local history investigation be seen as a group or individual enterprise? These questions have to be considered and the answers are likely to vary according to age and ability, as well as the nature of the investigation being undertaken.

Many libraries and 'heritage centres' and some record offices appreciate the importance of hands-on experience of original sources and have special study rooms where pupils can work under their teachers' supervision. The effort, planning, time and expense involved in taking pupils to the records must be weighed against the potential drawbacks of using photocopies of records in the classroom. A photocopy of, say, a diary does not have the same 'tingle factor' quality as the mud-and-blood stained original written in the trenches of northern France. On the other hand, a photocopy of four pages of a census return could probably be used in a classroom situation without problems. Most libraries will allow supervised pupils to use microfilm readers. This is a useful skill to teach but no more than about four pupils can reasonably use one microfilm reader – what will the rest of the class be doing? Using a microfilm reader and working with source material could form a valuable session away from the classroom, provided the distance and travelling time involved, the numbers of staff needed off-site, the quality of the material and consequently the validity of the whole experience merited it.

Written or printed source material can present particular problems, even if the physical state of the material is acceptable. Many of these difficulties can be overcome but teachers need to decide whether the time and effort involved in rendering a source usable are actually worth what can then be quarried from it. Handwriting, particularly from sources before 1800, can present a problem. Transcription is always possible – but by whom, and what would be lost? Language, sentence construction and vocabulary are often difficult, even in 19th century broadsheets intended to be read to the illiterate poor. Words currently in use may have had a different meaning in earlier days, and some local documents may be written in dialect or use local terminology.

Embedded concepts within local material can provide traps for unwary teachers and hurdles for the pupils. The types of hierarchical social structure frequently present in rural areas may need explanation; a study of parish registers may reveal patterns of illegitimacy which were quite acceptable in an 18th-century village but which may give rise to unhappy value judgements by some pupils. This could also be the case where mass baptism was common. Indeed, any local customs which require explanation can provide traps for the unwary teacher.

Some kinds of source material may require so much preparatory explanation before any meaningful work can be done that their value to a specific investigation will be severely limited, particularly in the time available. A tithe map, for example, could be used to show local patterns of land ownership. However, in order to explain what a tithe map is, it will be necessary to explain what tithes were, who paid them and why they were paid. Likewise, any document concerned with money, or weights and measures, will deal with the Imperial Standard, and some form of explanation or conversion will be needed. Care must be taken in making direct money conversions as the value of the pound and its purchasing power have changed so much. At all costs, teachers must avoid giving pupils a view of the past in which people 'wrote funny', could not spell and had odd ideas about scale and dimension.

This is not to imply that most written or printed sources cannot be used with pupils – far from it. Nearly all source material can, with care, be used with most pupils of all ages and abilities. However, nothing should be used 'cold' with pupils. All teachers are used to 'thinking on their feet' in the classroom and there will be many opportunities to do this when working with pupils on a local history investigation. However, there is absolutely no substitute for careful and detailed preparation.

A small-scale local study Source material of all kinds is the stock-in-trade of anyone interested in teaching local history. However, it is certainly unwise to try to assemble all source material relating to a particular theme before embarking on a local history investigation. The aim should be to begin with a limited amount and to build up a resource bank within a school or group of schools as and when new material comes to light. A photograph, plan and wage book may be all that is available in one year to investigate a local mill or factory; later, evidence given to a parliamentary commission and a diary may be found to shed light on a hypothesis formed as a result of the earlier investigation. In this way, a school's experience of local history can be genuinely historical.

The material that follows relates to a small area of Bradford, West Yorkshire, and demonstrates some of the source material that is widely accessible and reasonably comprehensible.

The large-scale map of part of Bradford in West Yorkshire (Figure 33) can, by itself, yield much of value. The type of housing available could be investigated, and pupils encouraged to discuss the possible advantages and disadvantages of back-to-back dwellings to those living in them and to those building and owning them; pupils could look for evidence of sanitation and water supply, and draw tentative conclusions about the general state of health of the area; job opportunities could be explored, as well as possible educational and leisure facilities. Many questions posed about this one source will, of course, lead to further questions and open up other avenues of enquiry.

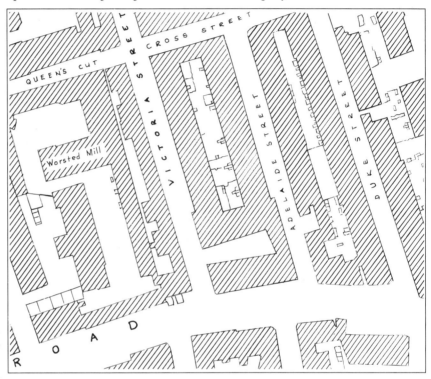

Figure 33 *A copy of an Ordnance Survey map of Little Horton area of Bradford, published 1851.*

The original map was published in 1851 and the data upon which it was based were collected in the late 1840s. Here the 1851 census, used with the map, can really begin to bring new life to the area (Figure 34).

Pupils unfamiliar with source material of this nature will need, initially, to spend some time on basic comprehension. For example, they will need to work out who was the father and mother of each family, the names and ages of any children, the occupations of parents and older children, and whether anyone else was living in the household at the time of the census. Having done this, it will be possible to link, say, occupations with mills and factories shown on the map; to place families in specific houses shown on the map, and to draw tentative conclusions about, for example, overcrowding. The place of birth of those living in the area will give valuable clues to population mobility. Histograms could be plotted, showing the places of birth of those living in specific streets – a skill which will link with other curriculum areas. Links can be made with the wider world of employment which would have been worked by the men, women and children living in the area.

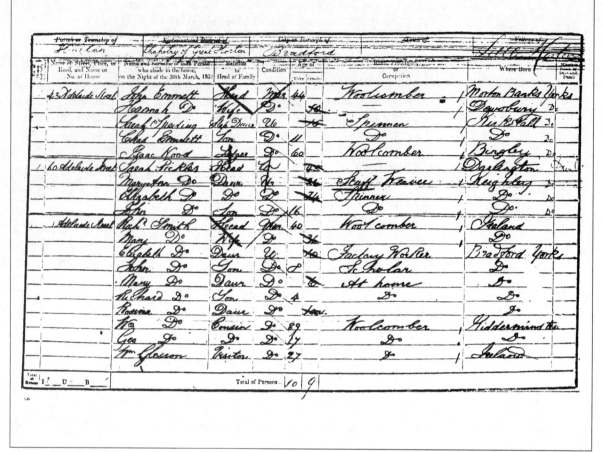

Figure 34 *Page from the 1851 census relating to Adelaide Street, Bradford.*

Large-scale maps and plans of specific areas and associated census data should be readily available to those with time to search them out. However, the discovery of some material depends on luck – or a helpful and knowledgeable archivist or librarian.

The report of the Bradford Sanatory Committee (Figure 35) adds invaluable detail to what has already been culled from the census returns and map. Tentative conclusions regarding, say, overcrowding and living conditions in general can be confirmed or confounded. The sizes of rooms and the number of individuals working and living in them can be calculated; most pupils will immediately spot that the number of available beds rarely matched the number of people in a family. Reasons for this could be discussed. The map shows the existence of a worsted mill, and the census shows woolcombing as a common occupation. Yet it is the Sanatory Committee's report which shows that the woolcombers in Adelaide Street certainly did not work in the local mill, although they might have been employed by the local mill owner. This sort of employment pattern relating to a specific industry could be profitably investigated, as could working conditions in local mills and factories for men, women and children. Here the wider context of the parliamentary enquiries and commissions could be explored.

RESIDENCE.	No. in Visitors book.	No. of Family.	No. of Apartments.	No. of Beds in the house.	No. Working in the house.	No. of females.	Sort of Fuel used at work.	Dimensions of Apartment.	GENERAL REMARKS.
Duke street, do. ..	23	11	2	4	2	0	Do. ..	13 0 .. 13 0	DUKE STREET is rather better paved than the previous one, but on both sides are filthy yards, and the public necessaries shamefully filthy and neglected; a vast amount of wretchedness is to be found among the inhabitants. The remainder of the circumstances are similar to those in Queen street.
Do.	24	2	1	1	2	2	Do. ..	13 4 .. 13 3	
Do.	25	5	1	1	2	2	Coal ..	13 0 .. 13 0	
	26	12	2	1	3	0	Coal....	16 4 .. 13 4	This dwelling is situated in a filthy and wretched yard—in fact the whole of the yards between Duke Street and Victoria Street, are unfit for human dwellings. There are a number of filthy cellars there, which are chiefly occupied by woolcombers. Those places are dark and ill ventilated—wretched beyond conception. HOLGATE SQUARE is a miserable hole, surrounded by buildings on all sides. This place resembles a deep pit —no chance of ventilation; a number of men and women work
Duke st. Manchester road.	27	6	0	0	4	0	Charcoal	15 0 .. 8 4	
Do.	28	10	2	1	4	0	Coal ..	14 10 .. 8 5	
Holgate square, do.	29	3	1	1	1	2	Charcoal	14 5 .. 10 4	
Do.	30	8	2	2	3	4	Charcoal	15 1 .. 15 0	
Do.	31	7	1	0	7	0	Coal ..	14 3 .. 12 6	in the cellars near charcoal fires. Seven feet below the surface. Workshop in a filthy and confined yard—seven persons work in this space—there is not a free circulation of air—the yard enclosed on all sides.
Back Adelaide st. do.	32	5	1	1	1	2	Charcoal	14 3 .. 10 0	The visitors give a heart-rending description of this neighbourhood —extreme destitution and suffering appears to be the result of their crowded and unhealthy dwellings.
Do	33	4	1	1	1	1	Do.....	14 0 .. 13 0	Very damp—no ventilation—privy ten feet three inches from the door—three persons work and sleep in this filthy and confined cellar, five feet three inches below the surface.
Back Adelaide st. do.	34	5	1	1	3	1	Do.....	14 0 .. 9 9	Ditto, ditto, ditto, ditto.

Figure 35 *From the report of the Bradford Sanatory Committee.*

The authorities have for some time been aware that the Chartists at Bradford, Halifax, Bingley, and other towns in the Riding, were arming and enrolling themselves in clubs, which they call 'Life and Property Protection Societies or National Guards,' and that these clubs regularly assemble, both in and out of the towns, for the purpose of being drilled in military evolutions, and especially in the use of the pike, large quanties of which weapon, it is understood, have been made in different parts of the district. Bradford has been the chief seat of these proceedings.

At 4 o'clock (on Monday, 29 May) the whole of the (Bradford) police force, headed by Superintendent Brigg, marched from the Courthouse; they were followed by 1,000 special constables, the mayor and magistrates, 200 infantry with fixed bayonets, and two troops of dragoons. This imposing force proceeded to Manchester-road, their object being to capture all the Chartist leaders residing there, and to search for arms. They met with no interruption until they arrived at the corner of Aidelaide-street, the scene of the conflict in the morning. There the Chartists had assembled in great force, completely filling the street, and when the police attempted to force their way a fearful onslaught commenced. The police drew their cutlasses, and the special constables their staves, and they were met by the Chartists with bludgeons, stones, &c. Each side fought desperately for a short time, but eventually the police and special constables were driven back, many of them dreadfully injured. The military, being in the rear, could not act at the onset, and the ranks of the civil power were thrown into confusion and disorder before the dragoons could be brought up . . . The dragoons having galloped into the thick of the fight, very soon terminated the conflict, the Chartists beating a pretty general and precipitate defeat. The police and specials then succeeded in capturing 18 of the most active of the Chartists, one of whom was armed with a dagger, and with which he attempted to stab several special constables and policemen. (*The Times*, 31 May 1848).

Figure 36 *From 'The Times', 31 May 1848.*

Adelaide Street, Bradford, did have a part to play in nationally reported events (Figure 36). Local newspapers reporting the same event could be consulted. It would then be but a small step to a consideration of the kind of pressure which led people into the Chartist movement, and to place the Bradford experience into a national context.

Planning local history in the school curriculum

The National Curriculum proposals for history refer to a variety of different approaches to local history. It could form a discrete study unit, be an element within one, be part of the course for another curriculum area or be part of a cross-curricular theme such as economic and environmental awareness. The following section offers some principles and strategies for using local history in schools. It is based on existing good practice and the requirements of the National Curriculum.

Local history in the school curriculum

Decide how the local history fits not only into the history curriculum, but also ideally into the wider school curriculum. It needs to be decided whether the local history should link closely to issues from another study unit. For example, a Shropshire school has carried out some local history involving medieval archaeology and focusing specifically on a deserted medieval village in the Clee Hills. Pupils were provided with extracts from a number of documents. They were then set the task of interpreting the landscape which involved solving problems. They took their own aerial photographs of the site by using a model aircraft to which was attached a remote-controlled camera. The pupils also had to reconstruct the village and its fields and use the written evidence provided as well as their own observations to infer what had happened to the village, when and why. This could easily link with the 'Medieval Realms' core unit when covering the defined section on medieval society; and, since the pupils were also encouraged to develop respect for the environment, to examine the local heritage and debate what was worth retaining and why, this study can contribute to environmental awareness. The technological problem-solving also permits it to contribute to National Curriculum technology, especially ATs 1 and 3.

Another school, however, may wish to divorce its main local history topic from the rest of the history syllabus. Several primary schools in the Welbourn area of Lincolnshire, for example, wish to focus on the Iron Age in the area, making use of a reconstructed Iron Age hut and building in a variety of problem-solving activities, such as how to survive, make implements and grow food. The schools aim to link their local history with technology, maths, English and geography.

Area of study

The geographical area of study should not be too wide. Pupils often find it more rewarding when they can investigate something in detail, rather than trying to cover wide areas. This is especially the case with younger pupils who find investigation of a large region difficult or meaningless. A street, village, part of a town or whole town often prove manageable. Sometimes an individual building will suffice if there is sufficient resource material. For example, an abbey or workhouse often proves suitable because a variety of source material often survives.

Sub-dividing the investigation

Individual pupils should not be asked to investigate too many aspects of local history. If the investigation being planned for the pupils involves a study of many separate aspects, such as religion, education, transport, employment, population, buildings and leisure, it is often better to divide the work so that pupils can delve into particular areas. For example, a Lincolnshire primary school has recently focused on its community in Victorian times. One class investigated a particular street in detail, another examined education, another entertainments, another local industry, another local individuals and their achievements and another the technology associated with its community, such as how washing was done and how food was cooked. Within a class the investigation was then sub-divided into small groups, each being given specific tasks. Another school divided its local history study into five main areas and different groups took on one of farming, buildings, the development of the village, the school and mining.

People and local history

Remember that local history is primarily about people. Thus, a local history topic which focuses solely on architectural styles, buildings or geology is not a valid area for investigation. While it is perfectly valid to embrace a study of railways or religion, it is important to remember that people were associated with railways and religion and these should not be ignored. For example, some local history taught in a Telford secondary school focused on the local workhouse, but the purpose of this was to examine the evidence to determine the thoughts, attitudes, problems and activities faced by a person in 1836 entering this particular institution. Two other points are worth stressing. Firstly, people include men, women and children and not just the first group. Secondly, local communities were rarely totally cut off at any time in history: thus local matters should never be seen in isolation. People in communities intermingled with those from other communities. This could be far beyond the shores of the United Kingdom.

Task-specific topics

The topic should not be too vague; pupils should be given a specific question or problem to solve. Some of the worst local history produced occurs when the pupils are vaguely asked to investigate some local aspect, such as the church or the town. This is often an open invitation merely to copy chunks from books, draw pictures or stick in postcards and photographs. While they might enjoy this and seem busily engaged, in reality they are developing few historical skills. One example of good practice relates to some work done by pupils about Ludlow Castle, which formed part of a staff development programme for primary teachers run by Shropshire LEA. It was designed to counteract the tendency for a project to be asked for on the castle and more likely than not produce plagiarised guidebooks. Instead, specific tasks were devised. One involved pupils working out how Edward, Prince of Wales, living in the castle, could escape and so prevent his uncle, Richard of York, holding him there. Another group planned a feast for the visit of Isabella and Edward II. Such activities were tightly focused and involved using observation skills, site evidence and other documents. It also involved technology, as other tasks included illustrating a new guidebook for the castle using IT, devising six visual display units at points around the castle, a tape to guide blind people around part of the castle and an electronic scrapbook showing various aspects of the castle. All these activities were successfully carried out with primary-age pupils.

Time-span

The study is often more successful if the time span is limited. Although some good investigations take place when the history of a community is studied from its prehistoric origins to the present day, a shorter period often produces better work. Much obviously depends on the area being studied. Sometimes the period can be very short, such as the Second World War. Usually it needs to be longer and 50 – 100 years is often suitable because it is usually long enough to detect changes as well as providing enough evidence. The last 100 years are often popular because they allow photographic evidence to be utilised. However, your investigation need not necessarily be limited to this. For example, it could involve a study of the local community in Roman or Tudor times, or during the time of industrial and agricultural changes so that the local history unit can be linked to core study units.

Problem solving

Consider specific tasks and questions once the geographical area, chronological span and aspects have been decided. The best local history produced often involves pupils having to investigate something in order to solve problems. It should rarely consist of finding out things and nothing else.

This is often likely to prove a difficult task, but one approach at this stage should be to examine the attainment targets and statements of attainment to see which types of tasks are likely to contribute to an understanding of the attainment targets through local history. The questions worth asking are not likely to differ much for local history than for any other type of history. Thus, tasks related to the following objectives may prove worthwhile.

Changes   What changes have occurred in the community, such as in the population, trades, agriculture, public health? When have these changes happened, and how quickly? Many schools are already doing some good work here. Younger pupils often investigate differences within their community, frequently over a period of about 100 years. Older pupils often consider why changes have occurred. By dealing with issues in a community which has changed over a period of time, the pupils are being involved in AT1. Some of the types of questions it may be worth asking are:

- In what ways are things different now compared to 100 years ago (the time is flexible) in transport or education or jobs or population, etc.?

- Which aspects of this building or street or town have changed since . . . and which parts have stayed the same?

- Which changes do you think someone living at the time this source was compiled would find most noticeable if they returned today?

- Which changes that have happened in the local area since . . . do you regard as an improvement? Why?

- Why do you think that . . . may have changed in the community but . . . has stayed the same for many years?

- Which people living in the community at the time might have felt unhappy about . . . (an event or situation)?

Causes   Why have things happened in the community? This could involve dealing with why the particular community grew up, why it developed in the way it did in matters such as population, communications, trades, buildings, leisure, life expectancy and health, family size and structure, migration, education, domestic life and religion. This would also aid an understanding of AT1. Some of the general questions which could be asked are:

- Why did some aspects of the community grow or decline or develop in a particular way (e.g. industry, agriculture, population, size of community)?

- Why did the population grow or decline at a particular time?

- For what reasons might a particular event (e.g. a cholera outbreak, a Chartist rising, increased crime) have occurred?

- What were the effects of a particular event or situation (e.g. population rise, a war, arrival of the railway)?

- Can you spot any links between situation 1 and situation 2 (e.g. the action of an individual or group of people and an event, or between the arrival of something such as an industry or police force and some changes in the community)?

- What were the most important causes and consequences of a local event (e.g. local enclosure or public health legislation)?

Viewpoints and attitudes There are likely to be aspects of community life which produced different opinions within that community – for example, those who gained or lost by a new form of transport or through industrial or agricultural changes. It is important to remember that communities were rarely united and speaking with one voice over every issue which affected their lives. Some consideration of this helps develop their grasp of AT2. One example of this which worked effectively at a small primary school near Gainsborough, Lincolnshire, concerned the evacuation of people to a local village during the Second World War. Pupils were asked to investigate the evacuation, and write letters to newspapers and journals seeking information and views about the evacuation. They interviewed villagers and evacuees about their opinions and produced a play focusing on the events and attitudes of the different people involved. A very large number of those evacuated were traced and returned to the village to share in the activities organised by the school.

Some types of questions relevant to AT2 which could be asked are:

- Does the evidence agree with a particular account of some event or situation in the community (e.g. the morphology of the community, particular buildings, life-styles, education, living standards)?

- Is there any evidence that the person writing this account, painting this picture, etc. of some aspect of the community (e.g. a local industry, life at a particular time, a street or part of the village) was being inaccurate?

- Which of these accounts concerned with a particular aspect of local history (e.g. crime, lives of a particular social or economic group, those living in the castle or abbey) seems most realistic?

- Is this reconstructed street in the museum similar to that researched?

- This is a general account of life in Britain at a particular time. Does this give a true picture of life at that time in . . . (the local community)?

- To what extent does this evidence about a particular aspect of the local community (e.g. police, poor law) support the following conclusions about . . . ?

- What type of source material might this account of . . . (a local event or situation or person) have used?

- Why do you think this account of . . . (a local event such as poaching, emigration, the fortunes of a particular trade or group of people, chronicle describing some medieval event) was given in this particular way?

Use of evidence   One of the real advantages of local history is the scope it provides for using a wide variety of local evidence. Local history sources stretch beyond written ones. For example, there may be remains of buildings such as archaeological sites for the Roman period, churches, castles and deserted medieval villages for medieval history, houses for the Tudor and Stuart period, industrial and transport concerns for the Victorian period. Other resources may be available. For example, if investigating issues within living memory, it may be possible to involve members of the community. Many schools already do this, e.g. asking old people what life was like for them in the Second World War, as a servant in a stately home or at school or to recall the General Strike. This often works particularly successfully if the pupils are involved in the process of preparing the questionnaire and talking directly to the people.

Artefacts are another type of source which can be used with local history. These might embrace all periods of a community from its prehistoric origins, through local Roman, Saxon, Viking and medieval remains such as parts of buildings, coins, household implements and religious objects to more modern artefacts such as those from early forms of local transport or materials from local schools or institutions in earlier times or those associated with the local community at a particular period, e.g. the Victorian period or the First or the Second World War. Making pupils aware of the variety of evidence for their community is helping their progression through AT3. This will be developed even more successfully if they use the different materials, interpreting them and looking for bias and inconsistencies in the material.

Some of the questions which might be asked are:

- What do these sources (e.g. written, visual, artefacts) tell us about life in the local community in . . . ?

- Do these sources prove that . . . (e.g. something related to the industrial or agricultural development, treatment of the poor, impact of transport, links with the wider world)?

- Use these sources to explain what . . . was like in the local community at a particular time (e.g. housing and public health conditions, leisure activities, the way the community was governed, the social classes or lives led by a specific group, e.g. women, the elderly, black people)?

- Which of these sources (e.g. written, visual, oral, artefacts) seem the most reliable/useful for finding out about . . . (e.g. transport, local religious life, crime, mental health)?

- Which parts of this source (e.g. parish register) allow us to infer that . . . (e.g. marriage patterns, mortality rates varied according to social class)?

- In what ways can these sources be used to support and criticise . . . (e.g. conditions in the workhouse, housing or lives led by medieval inhabitants)?

Planning Plan realistically – local history topics can run away with a great deal of time and energy. It is unlikely that a great deal of time will be available so one should not be too ambitious. This planning should include the methods used in teaching the local history. Some of the best types of local history produced at present involve the following:

1 Some input from the teacher providing a kind of background and introduction to the topic under investigation. It should never consist of giving some instructions to the pupils and then merely asking them to get on with it.

2 Clear tasks for the pupils which involve some investigation.

3 Some opportunities for pupils to discuss findings with others and with the teacher. Local history is an excellent vehicle for collaborative work.

4 Use of a variety of resources. However, these should not be excessive. It can backfire if pupils are pointed in the direction of a vast array of documents and asked to sort it out themselves. The quantity should be realistic and pupils should be made aware of the nature of the sources they are using. This may simply involve a brief paragraph explaining what the document is and why it was produced. Care needs to be taken to ensure that the resources are suitable for the ages and abilities of the pupils. This means checking for length, complexity and handwriting, but do be careful that the expectations are not too low. Evidence suggests that even young children can deal with quite complex source material. It is also worth remembering that the range of local sources is enormous and that it may be worth asking for advice on the range of sources for particular topics rather than constantly using the same range of sources such as censuses, photographs, maps and newspapers. Several useful guides exist on local historical sources.

5 Fieldwork activities which slot effectively in to the local history being investigated. One of the advantages of local historical investigations is that evidence often exists in the field which can be visited fairly easily. Although it is not always easy, site work can prove much cheaper and require shorter amounts of time than visits to sites much further away.

Fieldwork Fieldwork can take many forms and the nature and extent are likely to be influenced by factors such as ages of pupils, accessibility, cost and purpose of investigation. If it is defined as historical investigation carried out beyond the confines of the school, it can embrace the following types:

- Historical sites deliberately preserved and protected but not renovated, e.g. English Heritage castles, abbeys, palaces, listed monuments.

- Historical sites renovated to reflect a period in its former history, e.g. National Trust stately homes, private stately homes, reconstructed heritage sites, such as Ironbridge Gorge Museum, Morwellham Quay, preserved railways and canals.

- Historic buildings used for original or other purposes, e.g. cathedrals and churches, medieval town houses now offices, old tithe barns.

- Sites with few obvious surface remains, e.g. earthworks, deserted medieval villages or moated sites, old wartime airfields, Civil War battlefields.

- Areas with historic remains coexisting and muddled with more modern structures, e.g. streets or areas of towns and villages, docklands, turnpike or Roman roads.

- Sites containing objects useful for carrying out historical investigation, e.g. libraries, specialist and general museums, old people's homes, archives, businesses, newspaper offices.

The scale need not be large. It is not always the largest, best-preserved sites which produce the best fieldwork. Some excellent work has been done using very small sites, e.g. individual rooms in houses, a single grassy mound. Such sites can allow study in depth and be especially valuable when coupled with other sources, such as probate inventories and plans.

Fieldwork should never be done solely for its own sake or as a distraction from more routine work. It needs to be carefully planned so that it contributes to the whole investigation. The management is crucial and this includes the timing. There are often disadvantages if it is carried out at the beginning or end of a topic. This means that pupils will lack either context or opportunity for follow-up. Such activities are often suitably done in the middle of a local history topic. The way it is to be done also needs careful planning. While it may not be possible to do otherwise, reliance on a single site visit is not always the ideal. A series of shorter visits can sometimes be beneficial. Planning also needs to take place as to the precise nature of the fieldwork exercises. This cannot be vague. Preparatory work should assess the limitations and problems of sites and whether the site and nature of the investigation are more conducive to individual, small – or large-group tasks.

6 Activities should be planned so that they do not involve a great deal

of transcribing and copying. It often proves effective when pupils comment on the sources used and use them to solve particular questions and problems.

7 Some of the most successful local history investigations have deliberately set out to involve others besides the pupils. Participation by relatives and others in the community can usefully be encouraged.

8 Local history provides an ideal opportunity for a variety of outputs. Some work done in primary and secondary schools is of such high quality that a special presentation is put on by the school for the community. For example, a primary school in Lincoln used the four different periods of building in the school – the Edwardian period, the First World War, the 1960s and the 1970s – so that different year groups in the school traced the history of their area of the school, its pupils and what was happening in the community and the wider world at the time their part of the school was constructed. For instance, a man who came to the school in 1914 was interviewed by the children about his experiences, pupils inspected log book entries and registers, photographs were obtained and pupils traced aspects which best displayed continuity and change. The focus was thus on AT1. Pupils also investigated catchment areas, absenteeism, lessons, leisure and children's lives and clothes of the period. They devised an IT program to embrace the occupation of houses in the street in which the school was situated. This was put together into a display to which the local community were invited. Another school in the Lincoln area, which is built on the site of a Second World War airfield, investigated the history of the airfield, produced their own video trail of the remains and reconstructed what the original must have been like. Again, they targeted their investigations specifically on the changing nature of the site and the people who occupied the site. An exhibition was mounted and local people, as well as those who once worked on the site, were invited. The final product need not always be written, but it would be poor local history that never made use of the written word.

Also published by Heinemann educational

History Teaching and Historical Understanding

edited by A.K. Dickinson and P.J. Lee

Includes articles on evidence in history and in the classroom, language, explanation, Children's thinking, and understanding.
Contributors include Alaric Dickinson, Peter Lee, Bernard Barker and Asa Briggs.

0 435 80291 7

Learning History

edited by A.K.Dickinson, P.J. Lee and P.J. Rogers

Includes articles on empathy, historical imagination, the importance of visual presentation, and understanding.
Contributors include Denis Shemilt, Alaric Dickinson, and Peter Lee.

0 435 80289 5